Everyday SEL in High School

With this new book from educational consultan⸱ ⸱⸱⸱ ⸱⸱⸱⸱⸱⸱ ⸱⸱⸱ you'll gain practical strategies for teaching Social-⸱⸱⸱ mindfulness, movement, and team-building to hel⸱ contributing and compassionate citizens of the wo⸱ lead students through meditation activities, simp⸱ ⸱⸱⸱⸱⸱ ⸱⸱⸱⸱⸱ techniques, and other practical methods to help you proactively manage your classroom by meeting your students' SEL needs. Topics include:

- ◆ Empowering your students to understand their emotions, improve their focus, manage stress, and regulate their behavior
- ◆ Introducing your students to the concept of mindfulness and how it fits within the SEL framework
- ◆ Crafting an emotionally, physically, and mentally safe classroom climate and culture
- ◆ Engaging your students in activities to strengthen peer-to-peer communication, community-building, and leadership skills
- ◆ Providing your students the safe space to test their SEL skills through experiential learning, team work, and class discussions
- ◆ Honing your own SEL competency through professional development so both you and your students can get the most out of your school's SEL experience

This book also offers a set of Professional Development Facilitator's Guides to help you and your colleagues master the core competencies of SEL and implement them effectively across your school or district. The appendix provides additional strategies for teaching personal space, Safe Touch, and making mindful accommodations for students who have experienced trauma.

Carla Tantillo Philibert is the founder of Mindful Practices, one of Chicago's leading school Social-Emotional Learning organizations, and oversees a team of 20 dedicated practitioners who empower teachers and students across the nation through mindfulness, yoga, and SEL to create an equitable educational environment.

Other Eye On Education Books
Available from Routledge

(www.routledge.com/eyeoneducation)

Everyday SEL in Early Childhood:
Integrating Social-Emotional Learning and Mindfulness Into
Your Classroom
Carla Tantillo Philibert

Everyday SEL in Elementary School:
Integrating Social-Emotional Learning and Mindfulness Into
Your Classroom
Carla Tantillo Philibert

Everyday SEL in Middle School:
Integrating Social-Emotional Learning and Mindfulness Into
Your Classroom
Carla Tantillo Philibert

Learning on Your Feet:
Incorporating Physical Activity into the K–8 Classroom
Brad Johnson and Melody Jones

Motivating Struggling Learners:
10 Ways to Build Student Success
Barbara R. Blackburn

What Schools Don't Teach:
20 Ways to Help Students Excel in School and Life
Brad Johnson and Julie Sessions

The Fearless Classroom:
A Practical Guide to Experiential Learning Environments
Joli Barker

101 Answers for New Teachers and Their Mentors, Third Edition:
Effective Teaching Tips for Daily Classroom Use
Annette Breaux

What Great Teachers Do Differently, Second Edition:
17 Things that Matter Most
Todd Whitaker

The Inspirational Teacher, Second Edition
Gary McGuey and Lonnie Moore

Everyday SEL in High School

Integrating Social-Emotional Learning and Mindfulness Into Your Classroom

Carla Tantillo Philibert

Routledge
Taylor & Francis Group

NEW YORK AND LONDON

First published 2018
by Routledge
711 Third Avenue, New York, NY 10017

and by Routledge
2 Park Square, Milton Park, Abingdon, Oxon OX14 4RN

Routledge is an imprint of the Taylor & Francis Group, an informa business

Library of Congress Cataloging in Publication Data
A catalog record for this book has been requested

ISBN: 978-1-138-20783-7 (hbk)
ISBN: 978-1-138-20784-4 (pbk)
ISBN: 978-1-315-46101-4 (ebk)

Typeset in Palatino
by Wearset Ltd, Boldon, Tyne and Wear

Visit the eResources at www.routledge.com/9781138207844

For Rob, my loving muse, patient husband, and supportive thought partner

Contents

Meet the Author

Carla Tantillo Philibert founded the Mindful Practices team in 2006; the organization has offered innovative Social-Emotional Learning (SEL), mindfulness, and yoga programs to over 200 schools across the country. A certified yoga teacher with a master's degree in curriculum and instruction, Carla was a founding teacher and curriculum director of a high-poverty high school in Chicago. She has taught at both the secondary and elementary levels, is the co-creator of Hip-HopYoga™, and is a highly qualified professional development provider. Carla is also the author of *Cooling Down Your Classroom: Using Yoga, Relaxation and Breathing Strategies to Help Students Learn to Keep Their Cool* (2012), *Everyday SEL in Early Childhood: Integrating Social-Emotional Learning and Mindfulness Into Your Classroom* (2017), *Everyday SEL in Elementary School: Integrating Social-Emotional Learning and Mindfulness Into Your Classroom* (2016), and *Everyday SEL in Middle School: Integrating Social-Emotional Learning and Mindfulness Into Your Classroom* (2016). Carla and her husband Rob happily welcomed a daughter to their family in May of 2015 and enjoy long adventure walks with Little D. around downtown Chicago.

Carla and the Mindful Practices Team Can Come to You!

Mindful Practices provides high-quality professional development in Social-Emotional Learning, Mindfulness, and Yoga. Our engaging and fun trainings empower school stakeholders with the self-care tools to be the best educators they can be <u>and</u> meet the needs of their students. To bring Mindful Practices to your school or district, visit mindfulpracticesyoga.com or email Carla at carla@MindfulPracticesYoga.com. (Hint: Mention your favorite part of the book and receive a $100 discount on services!)

Bonus eResource

Carla and the Routledge team have created a FREE Social-Emotional Learning guide for schools across the globe that are safe havens for refugees and immigrants. This easy to use resource contains a step-by-step guide for educators who want to create an inclusive and culturally responsive Social-Emotional Learning environment for students who may have experienced trauma and/or are having a difficult time adjusting to their new school. This special resource can be downloaded from the Routledge website at www.routledge.com/9781138207844.

Acknowledgments

There are so many kind and compassionate folks who are part of this book's journey. Rob and Dottie Nola, thank you for patiently giving me the space to learn how to juggle (albeit not very well) being a wife, mother, leader, and author. I relied on loving caregivers to rearrange their schedules to take Little D. for a walk, sing a song, or share a book, to give me just a few more hours to write each day. Auntie Cathy, Precious, Maggie, Nana, my mother, Violet, and my dear father, Pat, your time and patience are truly appreciated.

I am indebted to Erika Panichelli, the vibrant and hard-working Program Coordinator of our Mindful Practices team. Erika worked many long hours to make sure the team was nurtured and growing. Our Mindful Practices family has been indispensable in sharing their wisdom, ideas, and feedback for the activities included within. I am humbled every day by the experience of leading such a hard-working, dedicated, and innovative team. I must thank my valued friend and research partner, Dr. Kiljoong Kim, for the charitable gift of his guidance and wisdom. He has been instrumental on the journey to deepen the strength and quality of our SEL programming. My tireless friend, consultant Anne Crylen, who continually inspires me to leave my comfort zone and who, along with the dynamic Peggy Collings and Kate Mitchell Alfonzo, took this book and worked side by side with our amazing team, Stefanie Piatkiewicz, Vienna Webb and Ericka Vaughn Byrne, to mold it into a rigorous and high-quality SEL certification program. Ladies, the magical combination of your many talents is truly what has made the certification program great!

As for the book itself, I am immensely grateful for my dear friend, and invaluable member of my Mindful Practices team, Peggy Collings. Peggy spent countless hours working with Emma Critchley and the book's editors to review the final proofs, diagrams, charts, and tables. Their hard work was vital in making this book an easily accessible tool for readers. Additionally, I would like to thank Chicago Public Schools, CICS, Conway, Berlin, Woodridge, Kildeer, Distinctive Schools, and our many fabulous school partners across the country for opening your doors and sharing your amazing school communities with us. You have truly given us a home to take risks and learn together.

To my amazing mother – thank you for gently forcing me to write my first book. (Per usual, you were right.) And thank you to mom, dad, and our dear friend Mary, who helped me assemble that first edition in our basement with the help of a plastic comb binding machine. Mom and Dad, I am forever in your debt for all you have done for me and Mindful Practices.

I am swimming in gratitude to my warm, thoughtful, and encouraging editor, Lauren Davis, her assistant, Marlena Sullivan, our copy-editor, project manager Emma Critchley, and the supportive Routledge family. I am honored to write for such an innovative, fresh, and mindful team and for you, the readers, who have purchased this book and supported SEL and mindfulness in schools. Many of you have reached out with thoughts, questions, or feedback and have shared these resources with your district leadership. Your support cannot be measured with words. Thank you!

Most of all I thank my loving husband, Rob. As the sleep-deprived father, tech innovator, and team leader (busy guy!), he selflessly cared for our daughter on weekends so that I could relax into the writing process. His encouragement, creative input, and patience with my "This is the final draft, I promise!" speech gave me the space to reflect and grow as a writer, mother, and partner. Rob, you are the love of my life. Your positive impact knows no bounds.

Introduction

After academics, what is the purpose of anything we devote time to in our busy classrooms? To help students grow into people that have positive relationships, are gainfully employed, and are good folks who volunteer at animal shelters on Sundays or help elderly ladies with their groceries. Isn't it that simple? If so, then devoting valuable classroom time to Social-Emotional Learning (SEL) and mindfulness is a way to empower our students with the life-long learning tools that will serve them long into adulthood, such as being present, responsible, bodily aware, and collaborative.

When I work with schools across the country to develop sustainable SEL and mindfulness programs, I often kick off our initial professional development (PD) session with a question such as:

> If you were to bump into a former student at the grocery store, would you rather she remembered the details of the academic content you delivered ("My two favorite elements were Strontium and Scandium because…") or that she had the social and emotional skills to be a productive, present, compassionate citizen of the world? Would you be more impressed if she could remember the protagonist's name in *The Old Man and the Sea* or if she was excelling at a career because she learned, among other things, how to manage her emotions and engage in healthy peer-to-peer communication?

When asked, almost all teachers respond that they want their former students to be positive, present, and contributing citizens in the world. However, in the next breath I sometimes hear an educator say, "Well. Um … I'm a science teacher. I didn't sign up to teach this touchy-feely stuff. It is not my job. Students should be learning this stuff at home." And, of course, we all agree. Yes, our students should be learning social and emotional skills at home, but in some homes they are not. And if they don't learn them at all, then they will never get a chance to use all that awesome science they learned, because they won't have the requisite social skills to hold down a job. Unfortunately, we all know that Ohm's Law is not needed to sit on the couch and play video games.

Now, this is a false comparison on some level, because as educators we don't want one or the other, we want both. We want our students to remember the protagonist's name and have the social and emotional skills to excel in life. To help them do so, we need to prioritize SEL content and methodology in our classrooms and view a student's ability to deal successfully with life's stresses as the litmus test for SEL impact.

Thoughts for Administrators

Do not be afraid to tackle the million-dollar question: how do you convert the disbelievers so that SEL, mindfulness, yoga, and self-care – together what I call Mindful Practices – can be built into the school's culture authentically across disciplines? This can be a challenge, as SEL or mindfulness often can be seen as a separate add-on that requires little or no integration or proficiency on the part of the educator delivering the instruction. Without integration or practitioner competency, the benefits of SEL can be limited and short term, at best. SEL and mindfulness are best implemented when they are integrated into the climate and culture not just of the classroom but of the school, so that there is a model for the students to reference. With the help of this book, you can be that model, enjoy a positive climate and culture, simplify your classroom management, and provide your students with the social and emotional strategies they need to be successful in and outside of the classroom.

When I finished my teaching certification in 2000, I left school having seen the term "Social-Emotional Learning" included on only one professor's syllabus. Mindfulness was absent all together. Many of the teachers I coach (from urban Chicago to hilly New Hampshire to rural Oklahoma) had a similar pre-service experience. All 50 states now have early childhood SEL standards. Still only four (IL, WV, ME, and KS) have standards K–12, according to CASEL. Mindfulness has had a somewhat different trajectory, but with the inclusion of yoga in schools gaining popularity, mindfulness is a close second, as the two practices are interlinked in many ways.

So, while the movement to include SEL and mindfulness in schools gains momentum, as educators we find ourselves in a difficult spot. We are adopting state standards for SEL content that many of our teachers are not competent to deliver due to a lack of training. To complicate the matter, they may be unaware of the gaps in their efficacy or lack the motivation to learn and share the content of their learning.

The classical paradigm of teacher-disciplines-student, student-corrects-behavior-because-teacher-said-so may seem to provide a well-managed classroom, but at what cost? Instead of creating present, compassionate, and empowered learners, it builds reliance on the classroom manager and their directives. Students aren't asked to learn how to be self-aware or self-regulate, they are simply asked to comply. In turn, students regulate their behavior in the short term, but we often see a resurgence of that behavior in a different classroom. Compliance may provide a school with great test scores and discipline rates while students are within their highly structured environment, but later achievement numbers for these same students (such as high school graduation rates) are often lackluster once learners exit the schoolhouse doors.

Thoughts for Teachers

Don't be afraid to dig deep! When working with high school teachers across the country, I often hear the question, "Why is Javier so well behaved for Ms. Munoz first period and is such a terror in my second-period class?" I refer to this trend as "teacher magic": when a teacher intuitively adapts her instruction to meet the needs of a child, but the strategies were never explicitly taught and the student ends the year without an improved sense of self-awareness. Often these students leave school without the words to express what positively or negatively impacts their learning or an awareness of how they learn best.

The Mindful Practices SEL competencies that are highlighted in this book – Self-Awareness, Self-Regulation, Social Awareness, and the balance between Self-Efficacy and Social Harmony – are skills we assume our teachers possess simply by virtue of being nurturers and educators. And many teachers do. These skills are often intuitive, as the good educators naturally "get" kids. They understand what students need and shift the energy of their classroom accordingly. However, some of the best teachers I have observed, when asked, cannot put this practice into words. While these teachers are effective classroom managers, without the words to explain their methodology, students may excel in their class and struggle in the next. The techniques in this book will provide you and your students the tools to find their voices and put your practices into words.

Given the emphasis on teacher Self-Awareness, this approach necessitates that we leave our comfort zones. This is not a program with the singular focus of merely knocking SEL off a school's to-do list. Instead, it is an integrated approach that calls on teachers and school stakeholders to Be the Solution by being active, present, and reflective. I have found that SEL programs that rely solely on teachers reading a scripted scenario are not a substitute for students experientially walking through the SEL strategies authentically in real time. It is one thing to read or imagine a response to a potential problem, and another to engage in effective peer-to-peer communication and team-building to uncover the solution collaboratively.

Where Do We All Begin?

We begin by devoting time and resources to develop administrator, teacher, and stakeholder competency and understanding around how this content influences the climate and culture of the school and, in turn, student achievement. If we expect all stakeholders to implement SEL with fidelity, then we must abandon quick fixes and find time for building competency with quality PD. Having teachers simply read a scripted activity or switch on some technology is not enough. We must move away from these practices as a Band-Aid® or something we do to "meet our SEL minutes" and look at these as life-long learning tools for both teachers and students.

Sure, buying a quick kit with scripted material seems much easier. But, if you are looking for easy, then you are in the wrong profession. Teaching, working with kids, is high-stakes. Doing something the right way, the way that we know has the greatest positive impact on student learning, is our professional responsibility.

Many of the programs out there conveniently focus on either the "SELF" or the "SOCIAL" component of SEL, for the ease of implementation. I am proud that our Mindful Practices approach addresses the school experience as a balance of SELF and SOCIAL for both the student and the teacher. As the Founder, I can stand behind Mindful Practices' work because it has been developed over a 10-year period in response to both student and teacher needs. My team has worked in demographically and socio-economically diverse settings to develop and refine the activities contained within this book. We have been testing these SEL and wellness strategies in the field, as boots on the ground, since 2006.

I present this Mindful Practices model to you as a humble how-to guide for creating an impactful SEL school experience. I designed these tools to help educators and school leaders implement sustainable SEL and mindfulness practices with fidelity. However, before diving into the Mindful Practices approach outlined in this book, it must be said that it is incomplete. As my dear friend Dr. Kiljoong Kim advises practitioners, for this work to have the greatest impact, we need to pair teachers with fields outside of education. We need to connect with pediatricians, trauma therapists, nutritionists, cultural experts, physical therapists – people who can help us, as educators, better understand the body's psychosomatic response to stress and how it impacts learning along with information that can make the material more culturally sensitive and responsive to the populations we are serving. These fields also have quantitative and qualitative practices to help monitor the work's impact on students.

The path outlined inside this book borrows ideas from some of the most thoughtful and innovative work in the field: mindfulness, yoga, cognitive behavioral therapy (CBT), trauma research, theater games, brave qualitative yoga researchers like Andrea Hyde, Peter Senge on systems thinking in schools, Brene Brown on vulnerability, Gretchen Rubin on happiness, Ronald D. Siegel and Jon Kabat-Zinn on mindfulness, Weissburg, Jennings, Greenberg, Durlak, and CASEL on Social-Emotional Competence (SEC) and evidence-based SEL, Charlotte Danielson's teaching framework (most notably Domains 1 & 2), Doug Lemov's classroom management strategies, Harry Wong's warm, organized classroom, and evidence-based best practices gleaned from John Hattie's work relating to achievement. I also give a proud nod to my own Mindful Practices team, who helped me design, implement, tweak, test, implement again, refine – and then redesign – some of the activities contained in this book: thoughtful activities such as Stefanie Piatkiewicz's fabulous Brain Massage, Ericka Vaughn Byrne's fantastic SEL & Mindfulness Matrix, Vienna Webb's relaxing Cool Down Breath, Precious Jennings' wise inclusion of cues to center the body in the Warm-Up Activities, Kate Mitchell Alfonzo's coaching tools, Peggy Collings' concise language for SEL and Mindfulness comparison, Lara Veon's mindful addition of trauma-informed teaching throughout the book. My fantastic mother Violet, a former principal who was one of the first to adopt our yoga-based SEL program at her school along with Mary Kusper, her right hand, and our dynamic Program Coordinator, Erika Panichelli, have also spent hours helping me mold and shape our PD programming so that it is meaningful and relevant for teachers.

I hope you will find our Mindful Practices approach both helpful and practical. Besides its innovative fusion of SEL and mindfulness, the prioritization of physical movement is one more component that makes this approach unique. I created these strategies to help develop your SEL competency and that of your students, along with practical implementation tools for the school and classroom. I encourage you to envision how each of the ideas can be modified to meet the needs of the population you are serving. Utilize these strategies to build a sustainable SEL program for your classroom, but, more importantly, take time to customize the approach so it is relevant and meaningful for you and your students.

As you dive into the book, please don't hesitate to contact me with questions or ask for me to come to your district to provide PD to your team. I love hearing from teachers, administrators, parents, counselors, and school stakeholders and visiting different schools across the country! You can reach me at Carla@MindfulPracticesYoga.com or through my website at www.MindfulPracticesYoga.com.

As we move forward on this journey together, I cue you to pause and take a breath. Even though we are the adults in our classrooms, we are not perfect. Moreover, we do not need to be. We simply need to accept ourselves in the present and try our best to model Mindful Practices for our students each day. The school experience is the balance of SELF and SOCIAL, which includes our calm days and our triggered days. It is our job to teach our students the life skill of coping with stress and anxiety as much as it is our job to make sure they know a quadratic equation or the structure of a haiku poem. As I say in *Everyday SEL in Elementary School*, it is important that we "give ourselves permission not to be perfect. The most important thing is that we try our best."

1

Social-Emotional Learning: An Approach, Not a Program

When I taught high school there was a student of mine, Roger, who couldn't concentrate on my oh-so-fabulous haiku poetry lesson because he was scared and hungry. I didn't see that. I saw a student that was disrupting the lesson I worked all weekend creating. Each time he fidgeted or talked I thought, "Ugh, he SO doesn't appreciate the hard work that went into this lesson. He is disrupting all the students next to him! I worked WAY too hard on this lesson for this little punk to ruin it. I should just photocopy the questions at the back of the chapter like the rest of the teachers in my department. These kids don't get ALL the hard work that goes into teaching. I should have been an accountant, like my cousin Mikey."

Finally, after trying to redirect Roger multiple times, I strongly disciplined him, as I did the next day *and* the day after that as his behavior continued. Venting to my colleagues later in the week about Roger (in a less-than-compassionate "I don't know what is wrong with this kid" type way), I discovered that his younger sister, Brandy, had been caught sneaking food from the school cafeteria. Putting all the pieces together, we figured out that Roger was hungry. His younger siblings were hungry. His mom, who had a problem with heroin and had gone on "benders" before, had deserted them and Roger didn't know where she was or where their next meal was coming from. Of course, my fabulous haiku poetry lesson didn't matter to him! He was stuck in the panic of meeting his and his siblings' basic needs with zero resources or support. This was coupled with concern for his mother's well-being along with hiding the truth so that he and his siblings would not end up in foster care. Again. Examining the climate and culture of my classroom, I realized that there were no SEL or mindfulness tools to meet Roger's physical, emotional, or mental needs. As an educator passionate about her craft, I naively thought that my dynamic lessons were enough to engage my students in learning, regardless of what was happening outside of the schoolhouse doors.

Witnessing Roger's struggle first-hand as an educator, I came to terms with the ugly reality that I was failing him. It was my responsibility to teach the "whole child," not just the part of him that I thought should want and to learn haiku poetry. Yes, the best SEL or mindfulness strategies could not have put food in Roger's belly, but they could have mitigated the crippling anxiety of the unknown. Without teaching Roger the tools to be present and ready to learn amidst life's chaos, his ability to excel in school would be negatively impacted. Thus, I fueled the cycle of dysfunction and poverty in which he and his siblings were enmeshed. If Roger did not walk out of my class at the end of the year with the SEL and mindfulness tools in place to succeed **in life** – and with the ability to write an amazing haiku poem – then I didn't do my job. Especially at my high school which boasted "creating life-long learners" in our fancy mission statement.

For Roger to succeed in my classroom, I needed to create space in my instruction for students to develop an awareness of their physical, emotional, and mental needs, so that he and others would be empowered to move out of "survival mode" (fight, flight, or freeze) and be present and ready to learn. Given the politics and legal restrictions of schools, a situation like Roger's is complex on many levels. But, at the end of the day, the lesson is a good one for all educators, regardless of the demographic they serve. If our students' basic needs are not met, they cannot be present and ready to learn.

This book fuses the practices of SEL, mindfulness, yoga, and connecting with others through team-building activities into one comprehensive approach we call *Mindful Practices* (see Figure 1.1). Mindful Practices are those practices that help cultivate awareness of body and mind so that one can operate with compassion for self and others. While SEL or mindfulness on their own do not traditionally include yoga, movement, or student wellness, Mindful Practices looks at the needs of the whole child: physical, emotional, and mental, as when these three are in balance, a student is able to achieve.

Mindfulness is an important part of these practices as its inclusion into the classroom setting creates "present learners," or students and teachers who are empowered to move through activation so they are able to focus on the task at hand. Mindfulness empowers practitioners to be conscious and aware amidst emotional, physical, or mental disturbances and distractions.

Figure 1.1 SEL, mindfulness, and movement in the classroom: Mindful Practices' two-part transformative process

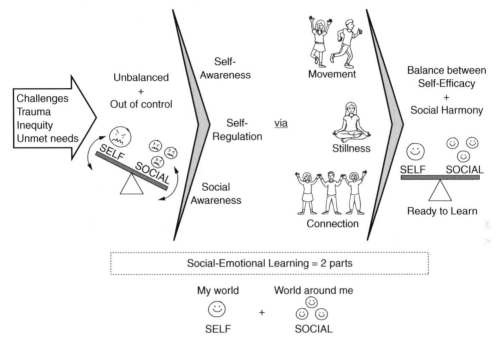

The Mindful Practices approach moves beyond a program that teachers merely implement, into a method of crafting instruction that meets the competing needs of the whole child. Looking at everything from a student's overall wellness (Is lack of sleep keeping a student from being present? Is a student's physical need to move his body keeping him from being able to focus?) to what drives student interactions (Is there a conflict with a peer that keeps a student's mind focused on "survival" instead of being present in the classroom?), teachers are given the diagnostic tools to look beyond content delivery. When we frame the implementation of SEL and mindfulness in our classrooms around creating a community of learners that is empowered to be present, we are able to overcome the negative narrative (test scores, "problem students," etc.) that is often preventing educators from teaching to their full potential.

This book provides the tools needed for the implementation of an SEL and mindfulness approach that brings practitioner and student into a compassionate and safe connection. We'll explore the belief that the goal of SEL and mindfulness – the ability to be present and aware "in the moment" to practice Self-Efficacy and contribute to Social Harmony – is a commonality shared across class, gender, and culture for both educator and student. For teachers to be effective, students must feel comfortable stepping through vulnerability into learning, creativity, and problem-solving. The Mindful Practices model outlined in this book challenges school stakeholders to stop viewing SEL and mindfulness practices as something that "under-performing children" need as a "special treatment" and to understand this as a collective learning process needed by all, because everyone regularly experiences stress, anxiety, and negativity. By shifting the emphasis from a handful of "problem children" receiving the services to SEL being a "Tier 1" intervention for the entire class, the Mindful Practices model outlined in this book will empower teachers and students to cultivate Self-Awareness, Self-Regulation, and Social Awareness through intentional practice in a safe and structured classroom environment so that the balance can be found between Self-Efficacy and Social Harmony (Figure 1.2).

These practices provide teachers and students with the tools to under-stand their connection to the world, how to positively express themselves within it, and how they can balance their own needs alongside the needs of the collective. When the school experience is reframed from the adult and child being in opposition to the collective working toward a common, inter-personal goal not only are life-long skills developed, but also the school climate and culture becomes physically, emotionally, and mentally safe for all.

The Mindful Practices approach utilizes SEL, mindfulness, yoga, and connection to teach the following four competencies:

1. **Self-Awareness:** self-esteem, body awareness, personal responsibility, emotional awareness, and understanding choice.
   Practicing these activities cultivates an awareness of SELF and shifts the learner from powerlessness to empowered.

2. **Self-Regulation:** adaptability, expressing emotions, managing stress, anger and anxiety, problem-solving, self-inquiry, and decision-making skills.
   Practicing these activities creates the bridge from awareness to regulation and shifts the learner from impulsivity to intentional navigation of behavioral choices.

3. **Social Awareness:** active listening, empathy, service orientation, and community-building.
   Practicing these skills cultivates an awareness of the SOCIAL construct and shifts the learner from a reactive, victimized mindset to a more proactive, communal view of their role in the world around them.

Figure 1.2 The Mindful Practices model

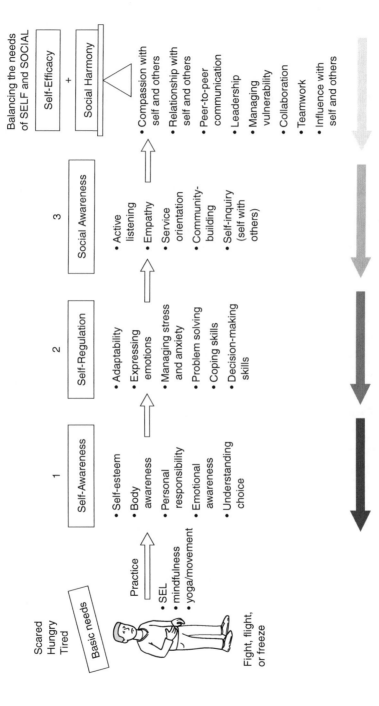

4. **Self-Efficacy and Social Harmony:** leadership, managing vulnerability, collaboration, teamwork, influence of SELF and others, understanding relationships with SELF and others, operating with compassion toward SELF and others, and effective peer-to-peer communication.
   When practiced and in balance, the learner feels centered, present, and like a valued and contributing member of the world around them. This competency also reflects the learner's ability to find her voice and balance the needs of the SELF with the needs of the SOCIAL, without projection, assumption, or excessive self-sacrifice.

When providing PD training to schools across the country, many school stakeholders express concern that the SEL competencies are often too vague for their students. By creating a chart of observable behaviors, educators can make SEL more explicit and concrete. List what behaviors "do" and "don't" look and sound like in your classroom. Begin simply, by identifying behaviors from each competency that will move your students toward mastery.

As I mentioned earlier, our high school students spend A LOT of time and energy learning and decoding their teachers' idiosyncrasies so that they can be successful in school. "5 points off if I do my math homework in pen!" "Drop a letter grade if I forget to put a heading on my science quiz!" "Any papers ripped out of a spiral bound notebook will not be accepted!" Some of these "rules" are spoken, some are unspoken. But, all are attached to expectations with consequences.

I remember my first Christmas home with my boyfriend's (and now husband's) family. I wanted so badly to impress his mother and be a "good" houseguest. I intentionally only took one helping of manicotti, and after dinner I loaded the dishwasher. I wanted to show them that I was "marriage material" because I had been "raised right." Unfortunately, it totally backfired! The next morning Rob told me that his mother thought I hated her homemade manicotti because I didn't take seconds and that I did a sloppy job of loading the dishwasher because I put the silverware "in the wrong way." (I wasn't yet aware of the knives up and forks down rule.) I remember how crestfallen I was and the wave of shame that came over me. I had tried my best and followed the "rules" I was raised with, so how could his mother judge me so unfairly? How was I *supposed* to know? What was she saying about *my mom* and the way she raised me?

Often because we were raised "the right way," we expect that social skill competencies are something our students *should* have, especially by the time they reach high school. We unfairly expect our students to have mastered a social skill that they may have never been taught, such as waiting their turn to speak, taking their hats/hoods off in class, saying "Good Morning" with eye contact or eating a "proper" breakfast instead of gulping down a bag of Flaming Hots before first hour. (Yup, we sell them in the school store, but then we shame our students for eating them for breakfast. Yikes!)

Let's recall my student Roger. Because of his mother's unfortunate situation, she most likely didn't teach him the social skills needed to be successful at the workplace, in a healthy relationship with a partner, or when dealing with conflict with peers. Because our role as educators is to create life-long learners (not merely teach our beloved content area) it is our job to teach the SEL skills that translate into a successful life outside of the schoolhouse doors.

Admittedly, we often don't know where to begin. (Can't we just refer the student to the school social worker and get on with our lesson?) Begin by being intentional and mindful in your approach. Your job is **not** to educate students on your cultural or spiritual beliefs, like all women should wear skirts to their ankles or the salad must come at the end of the meal. Your job is to give students the social skills and SEL competencies they need to be compassionate, present, and thriving citizens of the world. Many of us are guests in the communities in which we teach. We need to reflect upon our sense of "right" (knives down in the dishwasher – homework in pencil) and "wrong" (knives up in the dishwasher – homework in pen) and separate our own "peccadillos" or desire for "compliance" from the social skills needed to succeed in life, such as active listening or personal space. Create culturally relevant examples and observable behaviors so that students can step into Self-Awareness without shame and find their own voice around the SEL concepts. For SEL and mindfulness programming to be impactful, it must be explicitly taught and have a consistent presence in students' lives. Finally, we must remember to approach this learning curve compassionately and humbly, knowing that we will undoubtedly learn quite a bit from our students as well.

While there are many definitions or models of SEL out there, by fusing SEL, mindfulness, yoga, and connection the Mindful Practices' model includes a focus on the connection between a student's wellness and their mental and emotional state that often goes unaddressed in other programs. Our model prioritizes the connection between student's awareness of their bodies and their ability to be present, focused, and collaborative members of the classroom community. "I only had a bag of Skittles for breakfast and

I am having a difficult time concentrating on my reading quiz." Or, "I know I am anxious about my history quiz because my palms are sweating and my head aches." This innovative approach helps address the needs of the whole child by creating a judgment-free space for students to learn the lessons of the body and make informed decisions about their learning based upon that knowledge of their connection to learners' mental and emotional state.

You may find students in the "Does NOT" column (Table 1.1) who are dysregulated will complain of physical symptoms such as chest pain, fatigue, dizziness, migraine/headache, back pain, shortness of breath, abdominal pain, insomnia, and numbness who may have a psychosomatic cause. This process, called "somatization," is defined as experiencing psychological distress in the form of physical symptoms. Avoid jumping to the conclusion that students' physical symptoms only have a psychological cause (as there may be a physical cause that needs immediate attention). Instead, move toward a model of embodied teaching and invite the student to observe what is happening in his body and mind. See this as an opportunity to employ the mindfulness practice of noticing or witnessing one's experience in the moment without judgment. "Luke, I notice that you often have a headache before major tests in our class. Do you feel that is an accurate assessment of what is happening in your body? Would you like to discuss it further and brainstorm possible causes and solutions?"

Our model places Self-Awareness as the necessary precursor to Self-Regulation, with the journey of the SELF progressing from basic needs through to SOCIAL Harmony. The emphasis here is on the personal and interpersonal, as school necessitates that learners balance the needs of the personal ("I want to get an A on this Chemistry test!") with the demands of the interpersonal ("But I can't concentrate because Sarita keeps talking, which is giving me a headache. I want to punch her, but know I can't or I will end up in the dean's office. But, the teacher isn't doing anything about it because he is too busy helping another student who is still stuck on problem number 4. OMG!"). School is a personal pursuit housed within a social construct. To be an effective student, learners must astutely juggle both sets of needs – the SELF and the SOCIAL.

The Mindful Practices SEL competencies must be scaffolded and tracked, the same way we would scaffold and track traditional academic content. Just as a student must learn to add before he can subtract, we can't expect a student to regulate a behavior if he is unaware of its source. The balance between Self-Efficacy and Social Harmony (the duality between the personal and the interpersonal) is achieved when teachers and students

Table 1.1 Sample Charts: Observable SEL Behavior

Self-Awareness: Body Awareness and Personal Responsibility

Does look like sound like	**Does NOT** look like sound like
◆ Practicing "Safe Touch" (p. 178) ◆ Respecting your peers' Personal Space (p. 177) – No means NO ◆ Find your voice when someone is in your space or making you feel uncomfortable ◆ Use learner posture in class, eyes and navel turned to speaker. Headphones and hoodies off, feet on the floor ◆ Wearing clothes that honor your body and our school's climate and culture ◆ Making healthy lifestyle choices (eating nutritional whole foods, drinking water, getting enough sleep, etc.)	◆ Touching someone's hair, body, etc. without permission ◆ Touching someone sexually, violently, or in a way that is not appropriate for school ◆ Dishonoring our safe space by using physical intimidation ◆ Laughing at or dismissing someone who requests personal space ◆ Commenting on someone's clothes or appearance ◆ Wearing clothes that dishonor your body or our school's climate and culture (sexual/revealing, gang colors, etc.) ◆ Making unhealthy lifestyle choices (junk food, excessive caffeine or refined sugar, drugs, alcohol, sleep deprivation, etc.)

Self-Regulation: Expressing Emotions and Managing Stress, Anger, and Anxiety

Does look like sound like	**Does NOT** look like sound like
◆ Utilizing our POP Chart as you enter class to honor where you are each day ◆ Respecting our Agreements ◆ Practicing mindfulness, movement, or breath work activities to manage negative emotions ◆ Using our Talking Stick to create a space to discuss difficult topics ◆ Finding your voice ◆ Honoring your self-care needs so that you can be present and ready to learn	◆ Eye-rolling, grunting, or making comments under your breath ◆ Breaking our Agreements ◆ Dismissing your or others' pain, anger, or emotions ◆ Abusing yourself, others, or substances to manage negative emotions ◆ Dishonoring our physically and emotionally safe space by saying "Shut up," throwing chairs/backpacks, starting a fight, or being aggressive

continued

Table 1.1 Continued

Social-Awareness: Active Listening and Service Orientation

Does look like sound like	Does NOT look like sound like
◆ Respecting others' feelings, emotions, races, cultures, age, sexual orientation, and opinions so that all voices can be heard ◆ Using our communication tools, like Boom Board!, Pants on Fire!, or the POP Box ◆ Honoring our physically and emotionally safe classroom ◆ Honoring people with exceptionalities and/ or English language learners	◆ Focusing our attention on distractions, like phones, iPads, or food ◆ Laughing at others' feelings, emotions, and opinions ◆ Making negative comments like "that's stupid" or "what a dumb idea!" ◆ Dominating the group with your voice ◆ Speaking negatively or making assumptions about others' races or cultures

Self-Efficacy and Social Harmony: Balance needs of SELF with needs of SOCIAL

Does look like sound like	Does NOT look like sound like
◆ Leadership ◆ Managing vulnerability ◆ Collaboration and teamwork ◆ Being present and operating with compassion towards self and others ◆ Prioritizing self-care ◆ Making healthy lifestyle choices ◆ Using our communication tools, like Boom Board!, Pants on Fire!, or the POP Box ◆ Being culturally sensitive and respectful ◆ Honoring our physically and emotionally safe classroom ◆ Effective peer-to-peer communication	◆ Eye-rolling, grunting, or making comments under our breath ◆ Breaking the Agreements ◆ Focusing our attention on distractions, like phones, iPads, or food ◆ Laughing at others' feelings, emotions, and opinions ◆ Making negative comments like "that's stupid" or "what a dumb idea!" ◆ Dominating the group with your voice ◆ Speaking negatively or making assumptions about others' races or cultures ◆ Dishonoring our physically and emotionally safe space by saying "Shut up," starting a fight, or being aggressive

build competency by working through the stages of Self-Awareness, Self-Regulation, and Social Awareness.

Many schools ask me, "How do I get started?" Below are **five steps for moving forward** with an intentional and consistent SEL and mindfulness approach for your school.

1. Stop Looking for "Programs" or Quick Fixes: Craft a Data-Driven SEL Approach

Many SEL "programs" work great in one grade band, but are less effective with another, leaving schools with a collection of different "programs" instead of a strategic, informed SEL approach. SEL is an **approach** – it is a shift in the way your district, school, or classroom views addressing students' needs. It is not a program you purchase and say, "Phew, that's done, what's next on the list?" Be data driven! Answer the questions below before investing in resources for your district, school, or classroom. The SEL approach outlined in this book is designed to improve the quality of classroom interactions, academic development, motivation to learn, and teacher–student engagement through evidence-based, empirically driven PD and classroom curricula/activities that infuse social-emotional competencies into teacher–student interactions.

The questions in this section reflect the work I do with schools and districts across the country to align their SEL and mindfulness approach with their other district priorities, like academics. When I sit down with a new district partner, I always like to start with a "deep dive" into their discipline data, academic data, mission/vision, existing SEL programs – anything and everything that can make our collaboration rich and meaningful. We need to empower districts to craft an approach that is diagnostic, strategic, and impactful on the systemic level so they can move beyond metrics that merely measure "Number of Students Served" or "Number of SEL Minutes per Week" to evaluating the success of their district's SEL approach in numbers that reflect real needs.

While having all of this information is not necessary to get started, take the time to collect as much as you can. It is worth the additional effort at the onset to be empowered to make informed, data-driven decisions throughout your implementation journey.

A. What Is Your Target Population?
What information about your demographic can you legally and ethically obtain from non-school sources, such as Child and Family Services, city or state agencies, etc.?

- ☑ District-wide: early childhood through secondary learners
- ☑ Tier 1–3 students
- ☑ Students with exceptionalities

☑ Students who have experienced trauma and/or are living in traumatized communities
☑ At-risk youth and/or families who are living in poverty
☑ Most vulnerable children and/or marginalized populations (LGBTQ, refugees, etc.)
☑ English-language learners
☑ Parents, caregivers, community members
☑ Community-based organizations and partners
☑ Administrators
☑ Teachers
☑ Social workers, deans, Multi-tiered Systems of Support (MTSS)/ Response to Intervention (RTI) teams, Instructor-Led Training (ILT)
☑ Para-professionals, office staff, security personnel, lunchroom monitors, bus drivers, and custodians

It is crucial that you guarantee accessibility for all adult and student learners in your district.

B. How Will You Assess Your Progress?

What student-level data collection tools does your district currently use to analyze academic achievement, behavioral infractions, etc. and how could they be useful in this context?

When working with my school partners across the country, I often suggest administering the surveys or screeners listed below to create a baseline for implementation. Using a validated research tool is key to accurately assessing and addressing the SEL needs of the school community.

At the time this book went to print, many of these resources were available for free online. Prior to data collection, decide HOW the data will be analyzed and by WHOM (your school social worker or classroom teachers may not have the time, expertise, or resources to analyze the results and suggest next steps). Please note: I strongly encourage school districts NOT to use these tools as part of teacher evaluation.

Individual, Student-Level Data

☑ Mindful Practices' SEL Tech Tool (K–12th grade)
☑ CASEL Screener (5th–12th grade)
☑ SDQ (Strengths and Difficulties Questionnaire, 5th–12th grade)

For most reliable data, self-reporting assessments should be administered only to 5th–12th-grade students.

C. What Teacher-Level Data Collection Tools Does Your District Currently Use Around Teacher Evaluation, Retention, etc. and How Could They Be Useful in This Context?

Teacher-Level Data

- ☑ Mindful Practices' Teacher SEL Competency Survey
- ☑ FFMQ (Five Facet Mindfulness Questionnaire)
- ☑ Emotion Regulation Questionnaire (ERQ)

As an informal assessment, the professional learning experience is book-ended with a pre- and post-activity for participants (see Chapter 11) along with a SEL School Rubric (see Table 1.2) to create a baseline for each school's growth.

When working with school partners, we also use teacher-centered observation coaching tools and checklists to guide our PD participants and school stakeholders with authentic and meaningful feedback throughout the year. This teacher-directed and supported process empowers school stakeholders with the tools to track their SEL competency and develop professionally.

D. District/School-Level Data

What aggregate data collection tools does your district currently use and how could they be useful in this context?

- ☑ Discipline data: behavior referrals, suspensions, etc.
- ☑ School report card/academic data
- ☑ MTSS/RTI intervention data
- ☑ Data from other district initiatives
- ☑ University partners

For instance, Mindful Practices has a partnership with Dr. Kiljoong Kim at the University of Chicago, Chapin Hall, to help us monitor progress and outcomes, identify data sources, and set clear benchmarks that indicate progress toward our goals for student, teacher, and parent communities. By utilizing evidence-based practices and working with our school partners to identify appropriate data sources we are empowered to assess and reflect on the impact of our programming. As positive or negative changes are observed, we reflect on which strategies are effective or ineffective, make refinements, and share improvements with our school stakeholders.

Table 1.2 SEL School Rubric

School name: Academic year:

Committee members:

Stages	Descriptors	Timeline
5. Sustainable	**Ongoing implementation assessment: Have we created a sustainable model?** ◆ Thumb Check, POP Chart, and Call to Action are visible in and messaged around school. SEL is practiced daily in the classrooms and included in the morning announcements. ◆ School SEL + Wellness initiatives are sustainable and meet the needs of school stakeholders, such as students, parents, teachers, staff, and community members. Self-care is prioritized. ◆ SEL Team leads PD and Teacher Institutes that reinforce SEL practices. Climate and culture expectations of both classroom and school are clearly defined. Consistent SEL messaging and common language across school by all stakeholders and adults in students' lives. ◆ Communication tools such as the Agreements, Boom Board!, and Pants on Fire! are utilized across disciplines by all school stakeholders. ◆ Departments meet regularly to plan and implement end-of-year SEL Service Learning Project. Methods are developed to connect SEL practices to home and community.	School year ends
4. Experienced	**Ongoing implementation assessment: How have we grown?** ◆ SEL and parent Wellness Nights are thriving and gain momentum within the community. SEL is embedded in school sports and extracurricular activities. ◆ School SEL initiatives reflect communication between SEL Team, PE teachers, wellness stakeholders (social worker, nurse, etc.), parents, and school faculty/staff. ◆ SEL and teacher self-care are practiced during PD and Teacher Institute days. PE teachers and wellness stakeholders receive supplemental training. School climate/cultural pieces reflect whole-school SEL + wellness messaging. ◆ Departments meet to develop consistent classroom SEL practices and to begin planning SEL Service Learning Project for the school community.	8 months

3. Capable	**Assessment of skills learned: Where are we and what do we need to improve?** ◆ School SEL and wellness initiatives show thoughtful placement and are reflective of needs of parents, students, and community. Call to Action messaging becomes more common among school stakeholders. ◆ SEL and teacher self-care are modeled and reinforced during PD and Teacher Institute days. PE teachers, wellness stakeholders (social worker, nurse, etc.), and classroom teachers receive supplemental training. ◆ SEL Team meets quarterly. ◆ POP Chart visible in most classrooms. Wellness/physical activity is practiced 2–3 times a week in the classrooms. Thumb Check is practiced by some, but not all, school stakeholders. ◆ Impact of SEL and wellness initiative on school climate and culture becomes tangible. Teacher self-care is promoted and incentivized monthly.	**5 months**
2. Emerging	**Reviewing and refining practices and expectations** ◆ School SEL and wellness initiatives, including teacher self-care, emerge and begin to balance priorities. POP Chart visible in some classrooms. Wellness/physical activity is practiced occasionally (1–2 times a week) in the classrooms. ◆ SEL Team is created. A Call to Action, such as "Be the Solution" or "In the Zone" is adopted. ◆ Communication emerges between PE teachers, wellness stakeholders (social worker, nurse, etc.), and classroom teachers. SEL theme in morning announcements. ◆ SEL emerges as a theme in both faculty PD and school climate and culture. ◆ Parents are surveyed regarding interest in community SEL and Wellness Nights.	**2 months**
1. Baseline	**Establishing baseline, practices, and expectations** ◆ SEL and wellness are not practiced at school level. Palpable division between teachers and other school staff (i.e., bus drivers, cafeteria staff, building engineers, etc.). ◆ No communication between PE teachers, wellness stakeholders (social worker, nurse, etc.), and classroom teachers. No SEL theme in morning announcements. ◆ If present, SEL and wellness initiatives are random, inconsistent, and unbalanced. No common language. No consistent SEL messaging. ◆ Relaxation/physical activity is not practiced daily in classrooms. ◆ School/classroom climate and culture is nebulous or undefined. No "Call to Action."	**School year begins**

E. What Is Your Implementation Plan?

How does your district/school frame their initiatives (e.g., concept map, infographic, crosswalk, framework, strategic plan, backwards mapping, etc.) and how could that be useful in creating your implementation plan?

To enhance the SEL competency of both students and school stakeholders, implementation of direct service and professional learning must consist of skill instruction, skill practice, and reflection. Once the school stakeholders have received training, we ask them to engage in the cycle of inquiry of "Plan-Teach-Act" (see Tables 1.3 and 1.4 for tools) to continue to develop their SEL and mindfulness practices.

Student-Level Implementation

- ☑ As a "Thumb Check" across the campus: connecting adults and learners so that every student has the opportunity to facilitate a caring relationship with at least one school stakeholder
- ☑ SEL and mindfulness activities delivered daily in all classes through POP Chart Check-In (1–2 minutes per class period)
- ☑ SEL and mindfulness activities delivered in all classes when needed, prior to a test, when class is lethargic, when class is frenetic, etc. (2–7 minutes per activity)
- ☑ As part of an existing MTSS/RTI intervention
- ☑ Targeted SEL lessons offered in 12-, 24-, or 32-week sessions before/after school or in certain subject areas, like health or English

Stakeholder-Level Implementation

SEL PD services are offered in a variety of different program models.

- ☑ On-site (professional learning opportunities, workshops, etc.)
- ☑ Off-site (retreats, certification programs)
- ☑ In-class coaching/modeling
- ☑ Curriculum development
- ☑ Technical training and assistance
- ☑ Parent classes

In many schools I have worked with across the country, stakeholders are utilizing effective SEL tools across the building, but no common language has been developed and nothing has been codified. While there may be wonderful SEL and mindfulness practices taking place, there is no common language and students spend the bulk of their time engaging in a form of SEL code-switching from room to room, instead of being present in their practice. SEL may be called "SEL" in a student's classroom and then "Cool Down" when they go to see the dean, a "Wellness Break" when they get to their PE class, and then "Relaxation Time" when they are working with the social worker. While each of these stakeholders is well intentioned and, most likely, implementing solid practices, the students spend their time decoding what is happening in which setting, instead of embodying the practices themselves. This is why high-quality professional learning opportunities are so important: they create common language and practices across the school building.

F. What Are Your Projected Outcomes?

How does your district/school frame their projected outcomes? Are they normed with common language across schools/classrooms?

Often when visiting schools I will hear students say (after a situation has escalated and they have found themselves in the dean's office), "Dean Jackson, this is not my fault! Mr. Ramsey disrespected me! What was I supposed to do? Let him treat me *like that* in front of the whole class because I didn't have my homework!? Screw that! If Mr. Ramsey isn't going to respect me, I am not going to respect him!" Sadly, this scenario leaves Dean Jackson in the impossible situation of "playing detective" and collecting a dossier of information on how respectful/disrespectful Mr. Ramsey is as a teacher, instead of being able to unpack the situation using the established school norms, SEL outcomes, and expectations. By taking the time to establish common SEL outcomes across the school, we are empowering both our students and stakeholders to succeed.

Notice that the outcomes below are written for students and school stakeholders. This is important because it reinforces the poignancy of the "this is who we are" SEL school climate and culture.

As a result of the SEL and mindfulness initiative in [Your District/School] students and stakeholders will:

- ☑ Demonstrate SEL competency by effectively mitigating the negative impact of anger, stress, and anxiety on their school experience
- ☑ Find their voices and engage in democratic decision-making and leadership
- ☑ Engage in mutually supportive interactions and conflict resolution
- ☑ Connect with the school community via trauma-informed, culturally and linguistically inclusive interactions (including students with exceptionalities)
- ☑ Respect and adhere to our district norms for responsible behavior and collaboration

The SEL approach outlined in this book is designed to improve the quality of classroom interactions, academic development, motivation to learn, and teacher–student engagement through evidence-based, empirically driven PD and classroom curricula/activities that infuse social-emotional competencies into teacher–student interactions.

2. Fix the Problem of Practice: Develop Teacher Competency

Now that we know where we are heading, let's pause and assess our own SEL competency or what Jennings and Greenberg called in their 2009 piece, "The Prosocial Classroom," Social Emotional Competence (SEC). Intuitively we know that educators cannot teach what they cannot model. The goal of professional learning in SEL and mindfulness is to empower school stakeholders (including parents!) with capacity to apply appropriate SEL strategies based on context and need. Measuring competency of teachers in SEL begins with construction of an emotionally, physically, and mentally safe classroom climate and culture. Taking this approach one step deeper, the first step in developing SEL competency is creating space for teacher reflection and self-care so that teachers feel comfortable stepping out of their comfort zones and into vulnerability to avoid the burnout, hypertension, and compassion fatigue that often comes with navigating our increasingly complex educational system. Teaching is very hard work, and I have found that teachers are, by default, nurturers who will "run their tanks on empty" before thinking to take a moment for themselves.

The Social-Emotional Learning Teacher Reflection Tool (Table 1.3) and Flip/Flop Observation and Coaching Log (Table 1.4) are excellent ways for us, as educators, to reflect on our practice, assess need, and fill the gaps. If you are trying this alone in your school as an innovator, or you are one in a cohort of many, these tools empower you to take the time to reflect on what is working and what is not, so that you can approach both your and your students' SEL needs from a contemplative place.

When "running on fumes" becomes the daily routine, that routine becomes comfortable, and stepping outside of it is uncomfortable, even if it is healthier and better for all. Additionally, if the school culture prioritizes "busy" over "self-care" it is difficult for educators to step into self-care if shame and judgment cloud their vision. What if we shifted the paradigm? If we want our teachers to model self-care we need our school culture to prioritize these practices and honor their value. Teachers are human: they may get frustrated and frazzled and then fall victim to quick fixes,

Table 1.3 Social-Emotional Learning Teacher Reflection Tool

What does SEL look like, sound like, and feel like in my classroom?

This document is to be used as a reflection tool or to be shared with a thought partner conducting informal observations. This tool is meant to help sculpt an SEL approach for "problem students" or chronic whole-class, behavioral issues, over a three-visit period. This is a reflection tool and is NOT to be tied to a teacher's formal observation, unless explicitly stated by an administrator BEFORE the process has begun.

Teacher Name: _____ Name of Student Observed: _____ Was Whole-Class Behavior Observed? (circle one) Yes   No

Record each date in different colored pen/pencil/marker for ease of reference.

Name of Observer (if applicable): _____   ✓ Date One   ✓ Date Two   ✓ Date Three

Student Observable Behavior	Observable Teacher Response to Student	Teacher Physical, Emotional, and Mental Experience	Teacher Self-Care Practices
☐☐☐ lethargy/sleepy	☐☐☐ ignores behavior	☐☐☐ lethargy/sleepy	☐☐☐ **Physical:**
☐☐☐ low tone	☐☐☐ addresses issue as "whole-class" problem	☐☐☐ compassion fatigue	Day/Time/Duration:
☐☐☐ refusal to participate	☐☐☐ lower expectations for student	☐☐☐ overwhelmed	
☐☐☐ attention seeking		☐☐☐ frustrated	
☐☐☐ impulsive	☐☐☐ higher expectations for student	☐☐☐ addresses issue as "whole-school" problem	Outcome:
☐☐☐ talks out of turn			
☐☐☐ cannot stay in seat	☐☐☐ positive reinforcement	☐☐☐ addresses issue as "parent" problem	☐☐☐ **Mental:**
☐☐☐ frenetic	☐☐☐ punitive measures	☐☐☐ hyper vigilance	Day/Time/Duration:
☐☐☐ easily triggered/ combative	☐☐☐ threatens to take away privilege	☐☐☐ perfectionist	
		☐☐☐ sense of urgency	
☐☐☐ nosy/tattling/intrusive	☐☐☐ takes away privilege	☐☐☐ anxiety	Outcome:
☐☐☐ perfectionist	☐☐☐ send student out of room	☐☐☐ helpless/powerless	
☐☐☐ lacks motivation to learn			

continued

Table 1.3 Continued

Student Observable Behavior	Observable Teacher Response to Student	Teacher Physical, Emotional, and Mental Experience	Teacher Self-Care Practices
□ □ bossy	□ □ □ use token economy/PBIS	□ □ □ lacks motivation/given up on "certain kids"	□ □ □ **Emotional:**
□ □ defiant	□ □ □ give student "time out"		Day/Time/Duration:
□ □ constantly complaining	□ □ □ yell/raise voice	□ □ □ consistently overwhelmed by positive emotions	
□ □ chronically unprepared for class	□ □ □ shame/scream	□ □ □ consistently overwhelmed by negative emotions	Outcome:
□ □ easily distracted	□ □ □ non-verbal cues (flash lights, proximity)	□ □ □ Negative Nelly/downer	
□ □ feels ignored/neglected/ others favored	□ □ □ plays favorites	□ □ □ shame	□ □ □ **Other (i.e., Collegial, etc.):**
□ □ fidgety	□ □ □ positive side bar with student "You can do it!"	□ □ □ easily triggered/ combative	Day/Time/Duration:
□ □ chronically unclean	□ □ □ negative side bar with student "I am SO disappointed in you"	□ □ □ feels ignored/neglected/ others favored	Outcome:
□ □ no boundaries/personal space	□ □ □ movement break: whole class	□ □ □ chronically unprepared/ missing deadlines	
□ □ bullies others	□ □ □ movement break: individual student	□ □ □ defiant	
□ □ victim of bullying	□ □ □ Other:	□ □ □ not collegial/collaborative	
□ □ consistently overwhelmed by positive emotions		□ □ □ Other:	
□ □ consistently overwhelmed by negative emotions			
□ □ Other:			

Classroom SEL Artifacts	SEL Competencies Explicitly Taught	SEL Teaching Methodology	SEL Language Observed *Record examples of explicit SEL cueing, redirecting, student conversations, etc.*
☐ ☐ Boom Board! ☐ ☐ Pants on Fire! ☐ ☐ Parking Lot ☐ ☐ Agreements ☐ ☐ Daily Schedule (including SEL and standards) ☐ Student SEL Stories or SEL artifacts on display ☐ ☐ Talking Stick ☐ ☐ Thumbs-Up/Thumbs-Down box ☐ ☐ Movement or "Cool Down" corner ☐ ☐ Write and Rip ☐ ☐ How Might We (HMW) ☐ ☐ POP Chart ☐ ☐ Other:	☐ ☐ ☐ **Self-Awareness:** Day/Time/Duration: Practice: ☐ ☐ ☐ **Self-Regulation:** Day/Time/Duration: Practice: ☐ ☐ ☐ **Social Awareness:** Day/Time/Duration: Practice: ☐ ☐ ☐ **Self-Efficacy and Social Harmony:** Day/Time/Duration: Practice:	☐ ☐ ☐ **Vocalization:** Day/Time/Duration: Student Response: ☐ ☐ ☐ **Movement:** Day/Time/Duration: Student Response: ☐ ☐ ☐ **Stillness:** Day/Time/Duration: Student Response: ☐ ☐ ☐ **Team-Building:** Day/Time/Duration: Student Response:	"I see students demonstrating self-awareness and self-regulation skills by honoring their neighbor's personal space while working in small groups." "Students, what do we need to do right now to get In the Zone and be Ready to Learn?"

Table 1.4 Flip/Flop Observation and Coaching Log

Name of Observer:
Name of Teacher and School:
Room Number and Duration of Observation:
Date: Time of Day:

What the Teacher Is Saying/Doing *(Intentional focus on teacher SEL language and supports)*				What the Students Are Saying/Doing		
SEL Competency and Focus (Descriptors)				**SEL Tools/Activities**		
Self-Awareness Self-esteem, body awareness, personal responsibility, emotional awareness, understanding choice	**Self-Regulation** Adaptability, expressing emotions, managing stress and anxiety, problem-solving, coping skills, decision-making skills	**Social Awareness** Active listening, empathy, service orientation, community-building, self-inquiry (self with others)	**Self-Efficacy + Social Harmony** Compassion, relationships, peer-to peer communication, leadership, managing vulnerability, collaboration, teamwork, influence	☐ POP Chart	☐ Movement ☐ Yoga ☐ Dance ☐ Other	☐ Reflection
				☐ Pair/group work	☐ Breath work	☐ Mindfulness
				☐ Choice	☐ Other	☐ Other

forgetting that their self-care is an invaluable element of any SEL program's success. SEL and mindfulness instruction cannot be impactful if the canvas of the classroom is not clearly defined or emotionally and physically safe for the students or the teacher. The rationale for utilizing SEL across the school is about empowering classroom communities – all students and teachers – with the tools to take care of their needs by being present, focused, and mindful.

The SEL competence we have as teachers is more important than the competency of our students. As teachers, we are the delivery vehicles by which the information is conveyed. Our SEL proficiency cannot be assumed simply because we teach, the same way we wouldn't assume that all teachers in the United States are proficient in teaching Language Arts simply because they live in an English-speaking country.

If the Department of Education adopted violin standards requiring each and every educator to deliver proficient violin instruction, there would be an outrage among teachers. Administrators across the country would decry that we have not trained our teachers to deliver violin instruction appropriately. They would fear that lack of teacher knowledge would lead to unsatisfactory teaching and the spreading of misinformation about the violin. There would be concern that suggesting that anyone can teach violin without proper training would devalue the content and its delivery. And all these concerns would undoubtedly be valid.

This begs the question: if we would never think to adopt violin standards in this way, why did we do it with SEL, and are we sacrificing the fidelity of the practice in the process? We must move schools beyond simply adopting the state SEL standards or a mindfulness program. We agree that we would never just hand a teacher a violin and expect him to be able to teach it proficiently. SEL must be viewed the same way if we expect to impact the climate and culture of the classrooms in which the learning is taking place.

All that being said, state standards for SEL are a *big* step in the right direction as they move SEL from the realm of suggested and easily dismissed content to a core competency vital to a student's academic success. (And I applaud policymakers and CASEL for the countless hours they have spent advocating for this work!) The important next step is to look at the implementation side of standards. How can we develop our competency as teachers at a rate that meets the need for quality implementation?

I have found that the teachers who are most successful implementing these practices are those that find their voice with the work. Educators who can embrace the "split vision" between teacher and learner view the experiential learning process as the reflective springboard for effectively teaching SEL. If you are reading this book on a school-wide level, you might find the chapter on impactful PD (Chapter 10) to be helpful. It shows how you and your colleagues can work together not on just speaking the language of the content, but on modeling it daily to shift the climate and culture of your school building. Taking a cue from Charlotte Danielson's Domains and working toward "establishing an environment of respect and rapport (Domain 2)" by "Understanding your students (Domain 1)" is a terrific first step. By intentionally shifting the focus from "disciplining" students to creating self-reliant learners who are able to regulate their behavior, students are empowered to Be the Solution and Own their educational experience.

If you are an innovative teacher who is reading this book alone, bravo! You are the agent of change at your school. One breath at a time, you and your students will begin to witness positive changes in your classroom. By cultivating Self-Awareness, you and your students will be empowered to self-regulate and reflect on how your experiences contribute to the collective classroom community. While this, in and of itself, is great, your colleagues will slowly begin to witness the changes as well.

> "Hey Alice, did you notice how Butch's students are much better behaved this semester? I wonder what he is doing differently?"

Slowly a buzz will begin to circulate, and it is at this point that I encourage you to lead a little mini-lesson from the PD section (Chapter 10) at your school's next faculty meeting. Follow that up by inviting colleagues to visit your classroom during their preparatory periods to witness you in action.

3. Teach with Intention: Treat SEL Like Academic Content and Define Your Classroom Management Practices

SEL is for the whole class, not for the four "problem students" with Individualized Education Plans. *All* students and teachers, regardless of culture, gender, or socio-economic status, experience stress that keeps them from being present in the classroom. Therefore, both students and teachers need to tend to their self-care practices and identify the tools that empower them to be present and ready to learn. SEL and mindfulness practices need to be taught with the same intentionality as core content areas. One would never teach fusion or the Iran Contra Affair without pre-teaching certain concepts, and these same best practices should be applied to SEL and mindfulness as well. The concept of empathy cannot be taught in a week, unrelated to other SEL competencies. Instead, the material must be scaffolded (as shown in Figure 1.2), taught, and re-taught when mastery is not achieved.

By giving students and teachers a safe space to name their feelings we not only begin to omit the judgment and shame associated with the process, we also equip them with the tools to step into vulnerability and proactively tackle their stress head-on so they are empowered to be present. I encourage teachers to participate in the POP Chart Check-In to model this practice for their students. It is powerful for students to witness their teachers practicing self-care in an open and transparent way, and it is also the perfect opportunity for the classroom teacher to meet her needs in real time.

Many SEL, character education, or mindfulness programs focus on singular character traits taken out of context, such as "This week is empathy week!" These programs often focus separately on SELF (such as scripted meditation programs) or SOCIAL (such as group restorative programs) instead of bridging the gap between the two. Our Mindful Practices program authentically connects the SELF and SOCIAL through trauma-informed and culturally relevant opportunities for sharing, growing, and learning both as individuals and as a conscious collective. Viewing SEL through this lens empowers students to find the balance between the SELF and the SOCIAL in their daily school experience. This reframing guides participants to operate out of compassion for SELF, a skill that, when practiced daily, can help them operate out of compassion for others as well.

Good teaching is subject to compassion. Whether we are working with a student to tame his crippling fear of failure or if we are struggling to keep our cool when a challenging student pushes our buttons, our level of compassion toward our students can often be predicted by our level of compassion toward ourselves. Creating a compassionate place for learning means creating a space that is emotionally safe for students and teachers to take risks. Tackling the physical safety of our classroom space is often the easy part, as that piece is more tangible, more real. You can put a finger on "unsafe objects" or even "unsafe practices" in your classroom. The more difficult piece is the "feeling" or "energy" that creates the climate and culture of the classroom. Teachers must model compassion toward themselves and their students. An educator's ability to be compassionate

– toward herself and her students – is something that is felt immediately upon entering her room. It is a classroom where students feel safe, secure, and "seen" with a compassionate lens.

For example, if there is a student that always seems to disrupt the class and one day he is out sick, thinking "I am so glad that Jeremy is absent today! I will get so much more done without him in class!" is counterproductive for you as much as it is for that student. It's also only a quick fix, as tomorrow Jeremy will be back and there needs to be a solution that includes Jeremy in instruction. Also, although it is often unsaid, this negativity is sensed by the rest of the students and erodes the climate and culture of the classroom. One student being unwelcome in a room does not make the others feel inherently more welcome. A classroom that welcomes all, even those that test a teacher's patience, creates a consistent, emotionally safe, and compassionate environment for learning – or, as Charlotte Danielson's Domain 2 describes, an "environment of respect and rapport."

Be Transparent: Explicitly Teach SEL Competencies

Define SEL for students. Explain why you are using the Mindful Practices strategies (SEL + Mindfulness + Yoga) and what shift you expect to see in their behavior. (Hence the "Why" introduction of the activities in Chapters 7–8). Help students find their voices to narrate what their needs are and decode the choices that teachers and administrators make to help them be successful. School is equally a personal and interpersonal pursuit. To be successful, our students must learn to balance the needs of the SELF, such as test taking, with the needs of the SOCIAL, such as managing relationships with peers (notice the SELF and SOCIAL components of the POP Chart).

The secret here is to narrate the process for your students without using shaming language. Being a former secondary teacher, I knew many whose style was so military-esque and prescriptive that there was no room for student Self-Awareness to be cultivated. This is one reason some high schools often have great test scores and low instances of disciplinary infractions while the students are within the highly structured school environment, but why lifetime achievement numbers – such as high school graduation rates or job retention – don't follow suit. Students never learn to be self-aware or to self-regulate, they simply learn to comply. By narrating choices for students we are empowering them with the knowledge of what works for them as learners. Often, teachers and administrators are having these conversations behind the scenes: "Let's put Lamar in

Ms. Nicole's room next year, because she is a 'go-getter' teacher who does a lot of cooperative learning and he is a kinesthetic learner who has a lot of energy and can't sit for a long time." By sharing this behind-the-scenes logic with both students and their parents, they are empowered with the knowledge of what kind of learning environment is needed for success. I often witness schools making informed decisions about a student's academic trajectory, but not sharing the "Why" of these decisions with the student himself. So, when the student leaves that school (and the community that knows his SEL needs) where he has been successful and moves on to the new environment (where his SEL needs are unknown), he is unsuccessful. The student's only takeaway is that he knows that he "liked the way that Ms. Nicole taught." He is not empowered with the words to voice his needs as new environments present themselves. Transparency is key for students to take ownership of the SEL process and apply the lessons outside of school.

Exploring SEL and mindfulness "in real time" and engaging the classroom in experientially learning is the key to SEL, as it helps go beyond reading scenarios about what "should" happen, to dialoguing about and experiencing those scenarios in the present moment. This level of engagement expands the reach of the SEL practice through peer-to-peer communication, collaboration, problem-solving, and other vital life skills (see Chapter 9 on Crafting SEL Stories). SEL is, by its very nature, social. This material cannot be taught solely using technology, worksheets, or via scripted material. The balance of SELF and SOCIAL is required for the delivery of the content to have an impact.

As John Hattie notes in *Visible Learning* (2009), teachers modeling and discussing SEL strategies in real time is one of the most impactful implementation tools. Hattie also notes that social skill training should be provided "on a regular and sustained basis" and found that training was most effective "when interventions lasted for 40 lessons or more." Additionally, measured, predictable, and consistent delivery must take place over time, as Catherine Cook-Cottone's innovative work (2015) around "dosage" demonstrates.

Marry classroom management and SEL instead of viewing the two practices as disparate elements of the same classroom. What does safety and security look like in terms of the intersection of SEL and classroom management? In a word: predictability. Students need a set of rules and routines that are predictable so they know exactly what to expect. The rules do not change from day to day based upon the teacher's mood. A teacher approaches student issues consistently and predictably from the vantage point of an ally wanting to assist, not the arbitrary authority figure looking to shame. The SEL-informed educator sets firm, clear, and consistent expectations. But, instead of being emotionally reactive or shaming when those expectations are not met, this educator seeks prevention out of growth.

For instance, let's say a student enters your class and loudly slams her backpack down. In the old days, the conversation might have sounded something like this:

> "Renata! How dare you interrupt my class by throwing your back-pack around! You need to have more respect for your things and the people around you. I don't know what is allowed at home, but that type of childish behavior is not welcome in my class. Next time you come in here and disrupt my class I am sending you down to the principal's office. You understand me?"
>
> "Yeah."
>
> "Look at me when I am speaking to you, Renata, and answer me appropriately. Do you understand me?"
>
> "Yes."

Now, the conversation most likely sounds something like:

> "What is going on, Renata? Why did you just slam your backpack down? You are being loud and disruptive."
>
> "Adeela and Dorothy were just super rude to me for no reason. I hate this school! Everyone is rude!"
>
> "OK, well, I know that you are feeling angry and frustrated, but it is not appropriate for you to loudly slam your backpack down while I am trying to start class."
>
> "Fine. Yeah. I won't do it again. Sorry."

As educators, we have an almost preternatural inclination to protect our instructional time. In this case, Renata disrupts the start of our class period, which eats away at our instructional minutes. We don't want this to happen again, so we discuss backpack-throwing with Renata and feel our job is done. We protect the flow of our lesson, and we raise the students' awareness about a problematic behavior so it doesn't happen again. In this scenario, **the teacher also tells Renata what she is feeling instead of giving her the space to find her voice**. This is not SEL, as it does not build the student's Self-Awareness, it only benefits the teacher so the problem behavior won't continue and he can move forward with his lesson.

To practice SEL and move our students through Self-Awareness to Self-Regulation onto Social Awareness to the balance between Self-Efficacy and Social Harmony, the conversation needs to sound something like this:

"Renata, I noticed that you slammed your backpack down. Take a moment to Pause and find your breath. Would you like to share what is going on?"

"No. [pause] I mean, yeah. Sure. [pause] Adeela and Dorothy were just super rude to me for no reason."

"OK, so why did you slam your backpack down?"

"Um. I dunno."

"Can you Own what you are feeling?"

"I dunno. [pause] Frustrated. Angry. I mean everyone in this school is super rude and I hate it."

"It is OK to feel frustrated and angry. But it is not OK to be disruptive when we are starting our class or to make generalizations about others. So, next time you are angry or frustrated what can you Practice instead of slamming your backpack down?"

"Um … I dunno."

"Well, when you are at school or at home … What calms you down? What activities from our POP Chart do you practice during our check-in to help you be present and focused?"

"Well, sometimes I like to doodle when I am upset. Or, I practice Ready to Learn Breath when I lose my cool."

"OK, so how about next time you are angry or frustrated you take a moment to sit down, practice a few Ready to Learn Breaths and doodle instead of throwing your backpack around. Will that work?"

"Yeah. I think so. I mean, I can try it. And sorry about the backpack thing. I didn't mean to disrupt the class."

"Thank you for apologizing. Now we both know what caused you to throw the backpack, which is a positive step toward a solution. The most important thing is that you are empowered with a solution next time you are upset."

"Yeah. Thanks, Mr. Jakubowski."

"Any time, Renata. Reflecting and finding a way to Be the Solution is all part of the Social-Emotional Learning process."

In this final scenario, **the teacher creates space for Renata to build self-awareness and give voice to her feelings**. This is SEL, as it builds the student's self-awareness, and gives the mindfulness and life-long learning tools to **P**ause – **O**wn what is happening – and **P**ractice an informed choice.

4. School Climate and Culture: Create a Call to Action

Often, when I am visiting a new school, I will see signs for "Lion Pride," "Warrior Pride," or "Whatever-the-school-mascot-happens-to-be Pride." I will walk the halls and hear teachers witnessing "Lion Pride" among the students. When I stop to ask a student what it means to be a Lincoln Lion, the student will often respond with a comment about the reward, not the observable behavior. "Being a 'good' Lincoln Lion means I get to go to the school store to get a bag of Flaming Hots."

This is problematic. Yes, we could enter into the age-old debate in education over intrinsic versus extrinsic motivation in school, but I would argue the problem isn't with the Flaming Hots (although it must be said that incentivizing junk food at a school is an unhealthy practice). No, it is with the lack of clear messaging from the school site. What does the school stand for? It can't be a bag of Flaming Hots, right?

What does your school stand for, and how can a Call to Action, or an instruction that begets an immediate response, be developed to communicate that rallying cry to all stakeholders in the building? What does *your Call to Action* look, sound, and feel like at your school? Is it about empowering classroom communities – all students and teachers – with the tools to succeed at life?

When I was finalizing this section of the book I was working on the East Coast with a school district close to my heart, Conway, New Hampshire. They have a truly fantastic principal, dedicated teachers, and stellar SEL happening in certain classrooms, but the need to extend the practices across grade levels and outside of the schoolhouse doors had not been met. So Principal Hastings and I worked hand in hand to develop a simple, no-nonsense Call to Action that would speak to his students, teachers, and school community: Being In the Zone. Given its use in sports, this phrasing was familiar and catchy enough that his school community could easily adopt it.

Being In the Zone translated to being ready – whether it was ready to take a math test, ready to Be the Solution and resolve a conflict, or ready for the big game after school, a state of readiness became the rallying cry.

The state of readiness, or being present in the moment, is the same end goal as practicing mindfulness. Cueing the students to "Be In the Zone" helps them cultivate the awareness needed to shut out internal and external clutter so that they can be present and ready for the task at hand.

A Call to Action frames every problem or issue the students encounter as an opportunity to positively move a situation forward or contribute to the classroom community. "Fernando, what do you need to do to Get In the Zone, stop distracting the students next to you and focus on your writing prompt?"

Be the Solution, Being In the Zone, or whatever Call to Action is implemented, should work in all settings: classroom, lunchroom, on the bus, lining up, and should be spoken by all school stakeholders. "Lori Ann, are we Being the Solution right now by using our cell phone in line?"

The Call to Action becomes a phrase heard round the school, messaged by every adult. SEL is no longer a sidebar add-on. It is a phrase, a code, a vital organ of the school culture. If I were visiting your school, I would hear the assistant principal use the Call to Action with a student in his office, I would hear the PE teacher use it with a student he had pulled to the side for a quick behavioral chat, I would hear the woman running the lunch program use it with a student who was throwing a carrot, I would hear the bus driver use it to praise a student who stayed in his seat, I would hear the parent coordinator use it to rally a group of disgruntled parents at the PTA meeting, I would hear a parent saying it to their child as he leaves the court after a tough loss, I would hear the principal use it to recognize her teachers Being the Solution at the faculty meeting. It rings throughout the school. It shifts the focus from being stuck in the problem to finding a solution and, most importantly, owning how that solution impacts both the personal and interpersonal aspect of school for students, teachers, parents, and administrators (Figure 1.3).

Peter Senge's work around schools as systems reinforces that educators should take their thinking to the larger, whole-school scale. For instance, "What can we, as the educators and stakeholders of Nola High School, communicate across and within the system to define it?"

If an SEL program at a school is going to have any weight, schools need to stand for something and, as Senge notes, that something needs to be indicative of the larger system in which the school is housed. To cultivate that magical balance between Self-Efficacy and Social Harmony, students must feel that their actions impact that system. "Good" and "Bad" behavior cannot simply be defined by the classroom the students happen to be in at that moment, or else our students spend their time decoding the teacher's quirks instead of learning to be accountable to the larger school community.

Figure 1.3 Your school's successful SEL communication

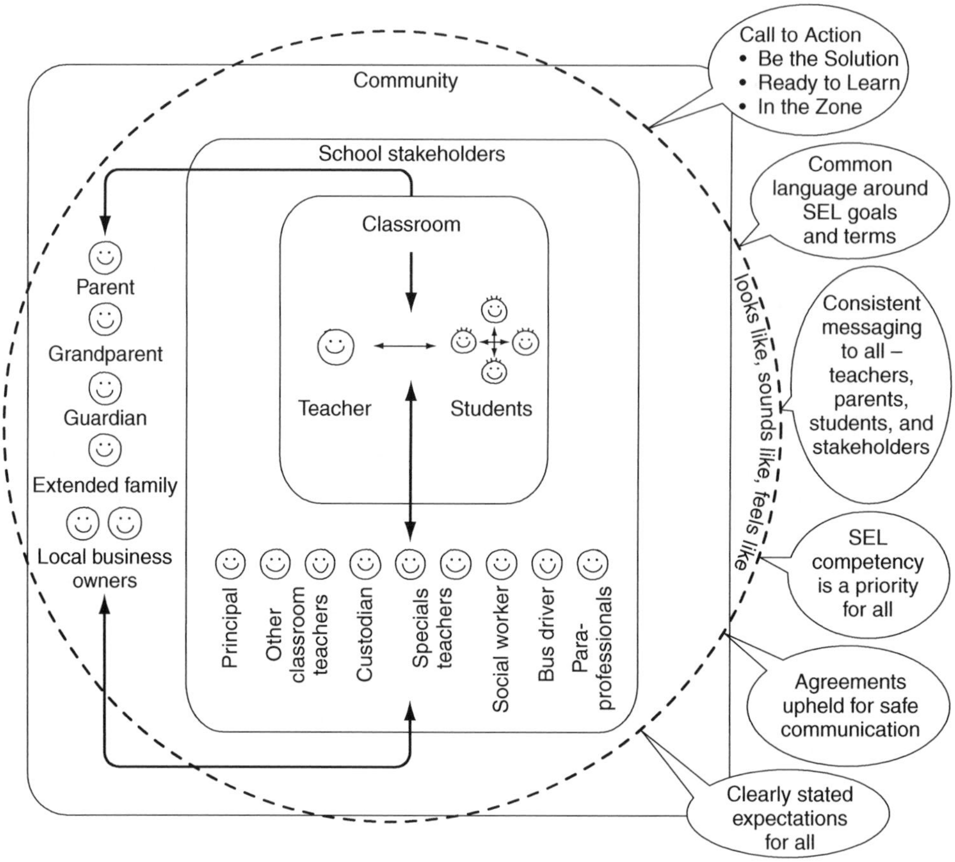

"In Ms. Divito's Art room I can't write in pen, or else she gets mad. But she is fine if we don't raise our hands when we want to talk. In Mrs. Dixon's English class I must write in pen, but I have to put a heading on the paper and raise my hand if I want to talk. In Mr. Burr's advisory period, we can write in whatever we want but we have to hold up two fingers if we have a question instead of raising our hand."

Yes, we expect our students to keep track of all this and to be able to regulate their behavior, communicate with peers, and be present and ready to learn as well! It is no wonder when I ask students what Lion Pride is, their minds go to the reward. The behavioral expectations are a jumbled, random mess with personal preference as the only rationale. We want students to be able to demonstrate the values of the Call to Action – to show that they know why they are here, what is expected of them, why it matters if they behave, and what we are all here to do – together. "Being a Lincoln Lion means that I am In the Zone, that I am a focused and accountable member of my school community."

The dual focus – on the SELF and the SOCIAL concurrently – is at the heart of the Mindful Practices' SEL approach. It cannot just be "empathy week" or SEL time on Wednesday morning and *that* is when students' minds are on Being In the Zone or Being the Solution. From the moment the principal opens the building the school experience is viewed, for all, through the Be the Solution lens. If someone is not Being the Solution – meaning she is stuck in a scarcity mindset, thinking only of problems and not of solutions – then Be the Solution is the rallying cry, the Call to Action, to shift her thinking back to what is best for the school or classroom community.

The first step for successful implementation is to build consensus on an appropriate Call to Action that is inclusive, meaningful, and culturally relevant for your school community. Develop common language and message it to teachers, parents, students, and community members. Give examples of what it is and what it is not. Provide school stakeholders with ample PD so that they can not only help you develop it but also take ownership of it and implement it with fidelity. Include parents and auxiliary staff in the initiative, and remind them that they are, as adult presences in our students' lives, role models.

When implementing SEL in her school, the dynamic Chicago Public Schools (CPS) principal, Jenn Farrell-Rottman, assigned each and every high school student in her building to an adult to "have their back." This adult had weekly before/after school check-ins with the student or took an extra moment in class to connect with him or her, so each student in the building had "a trusting relationship with at least one adult in the school" (Chicago Public Schools (CPS) 2017). To help facilitate a similar process, my friend Greg Wolcott, an Assistant Superintendent in Woodridge School District, prints out a copy of all the students' badges and keeps them in the faculty lounge. Greg tells his team that by the third week of school all the students must be "claimed" or they will be assigned to school stakeholders across the building. Not only does this help motivate adults to be part of this initiative, it also opens the process up to adults outside of the classroom, like security personnel, deans, or coaches who are often the first or last person a student comes into contact with over the course of a school day.

5. Name the Elephant in the Room: Basic Needs Trump Learning

Harking back to Roger's story at the beginning of this chapter, there are multiple reasons to prioritize wellness in schools, but the first is that teachers need to be empowered to model healthy practices for students so that the school community is healthy and well. If students are thirsty, we want them to reach for water, not soda. If students are hungry, we want them to reach for almonds, not potato chips. We want students to make the connection between what they put into their bodies and how their bodies and minds function. Are they more present and ready to learn after a candy bar or a bag of baby carrots? How do sleeping, eating, drinking, stress, and exercise impact them as learners?

An additional layer to the wellness piece is being aware of our many students whose basic needs are not met. This includes not just food and shelter, but also access to a private bed, shower, and clean clothes. How do we, as educators who are with them 8 hours a day, help them strategize positive solutions for being hungry, tired, or unshowered in our classrooms? When Terrice is falling asleep in class for the fifth day in a row, do we nudge him and say, "Sleeping is for home, not for school" and simply leave it at that? When Amy is sneaking sunflower seeds out of her pocket during your first hour math class, do you simply give her an unforgiving "put it away" look or do you check in with her to investigate if she made it for school breakfast this morning? As I outline on p. 11, students' ability to cultivate Self-Awareness and Self-Regulation is compromised when they are stuck in the panic of meeting their basic needs. As adults, we are the same way; we just have more resources to counter the anxiety of our basic needs not being met. If we had a restless night's sleep, we just swing by the faculty lounge for a cup of coffee. Many of our students live in poverty where being hungry, tired, and having no option but dirty clothes is a daily reality. Their resources are limited and so school becomes the place that not only helps fill the gaps, but models healthy lifestyle choices that our students may not have access to at home.

If we unpack "student health and wellness" a bit further we see that there are two essential questions to ask ourselves daily: Are our students basic needs met? Are we taking responsibility for modeling healthy lifestyle choices?

This topic is a sensitive one and I have often heard teachers say, "Geez, really!? I have to worry about teaching these kids The Battle of Bunker Hill *and* worry about whether or not they have had breakfast or more than 3 hours' sleep? Isn't this basic needs stuff the parents' job?" *Yes*. It is the parents' job. But if the students are not learning the skills to manage these needs at home, how will they be able to counter the negative impact not only on their learning but on their life's journey as well?

As educators, it is important that we do everything we can to model healthy practices throughout the school day, especially for students who are making very adult decisions when dealing with life outside the classroom. Some of our students are given money to buy their own breakfast at the corner store before school for themselves and their siblings. This decision requires that students understand that sugar, caffeine, and nutritionally void foods negatively impact their learning. As parents are often not able to do this, for myriad reasons, the best way to communicate healthy lifestyle choices – what to eat, what to drink, methods of exercise, ways to deal with stress, socially appropriate hygiene – is through teacher modeling.

As America is topping the charts as one of the most obese countries in the world, asking teachers to model healthy choices can often be a delicate topic as teachers may be struggling with defining health and wellness for themselves. That being said, it is time for schools to draw a line in the sand: x is a healthy practice to model in front of students, y is not. If we agree that teachers are powerful role models and that consuming candy and junk food is an unhealthy practice, then we must also agree that teachers should not model or encourage unhealthy practices in front of students or their families (*even* in the case of fundraising or the school store). Drawing that line begets difficult conversations, because, just like SEL, not all adults are self-aware of what is or is not a practice that is healthy and safe for the classroom. When in question, bring it back to your school's Call to Action. Every practice in the school building should help your students Be In the Zone, be present, and be Ready to Learn.

2

Connecting SEL and Mindfulness

Between stimulus and response there is a space. In that space is our power to choose our response. In our response lies our growth and our freedom.

Viktor E. Frankl

As educators we don't have favorite students, of course. But, I remember one, Javier or "Javie," that I had a particular soft spot for in my high school history class. Javie had a rough time at home – his dad was not around, and his mom was 15 when she had him, so Javie was treated more like a sibling than a child. His house was a chaotic place with a TV always blaring and meals consisting of chips, soda, and candy. He often came to school hungry or having slept in his clothes. From conversations with the school social worker I knew Javie had witnessed his mother get "roughed up" by her off-and-on alcoholic boyfriend a few times and that Javie often found himself sleeping on friends' couches in lieu of coming home. There was little "quiet" or "structure" in Javie's life and so sitting still and working within a structured environment were two competencies with which he consistently struggled.

Even with all the challenges he faced, Javie was the light of our class. He excelled at group work, kinesthetic learning, or any sort of "roll up your sleeves and collaborate with peers on a project" type assignment. But, the sense of humor and gregarious personality that helped Javie thrive in a group setting, also made him a struggle during classroom activities that required stillness, like test taking or silent work.

It never failed, the minute I finally got the class to be quiet Javie talked out of turn, sent a paper football flying across the class, or interrupted our lesson with a non-instructional question like, "Why is our mascot a lynx? Nobody even knows what a lynx is. How stupid, man!" Exasperated I would turn to him with pleading eyes and say, "Javie, why did you just do that? We just talked about talking out of turn *yesterday*!" He would invariably look up at me and say, "I dunno, Ms. T. I'm sorry."

Was he lying to me? Did he know why it was uncomfortable for him to sit still or to focus or be comfortable in quiet? No. In the chaos of Javie's life, he had never been given the time to learn the space "between stimulus and response" so that he could self-regulate. His actions lorded over him. He had never had the opportunity to cultivate an awareness of his actions, he was simply disciplined or taken to the office.

I knew that Javie was coping with stress, anxiety, and negativity in his life, but as a new teacher without SEL or mindfulness tools in my toolbox yet, I often felt ineffective in coaching him how to be the student I needed him to be to succeed in my class. Some students may be dealing with the pain of living in poverty, some may be dealing with the stressors of a fiercely competitive academic environment, and others, like Javie and Roger, may be coping with a tough home life that negatively impacts their ability to focus on the present moment and learn.

Enter mindfulness instruction! Mindfulness instruction – with its grace, simplicity, and ease – creates the vehicle through which students can cultivate comfort in quiet so that they are empowered to step into Self-Awareness and Self-Regulation.

What Is Mindfulness?

According to Mark Williams at the University of Oxford, "Mindfulness means non-judgmental awareness. A direct knowing of what is going on inside and outside of ourselves, moment by moment." Or, as Jon Kabat-Zinn simply states, "The awareness that emerges through paying attention on purpose."

Mindfulness practices give learners the tools to be present – be in the moment, without fear, shame, or judgment of self or others. Practicing mindfulness in schools gives the students the tools to mitigate the factors that often negatively impact learning (hunger, fear, pain) so they are empowered to be present and ready to learn – about themselves, their peers, and your academic content. Table 2.1 is a diagram created by my

Table 2.1 Mindfulness Competencies Matched with Corresponding Social-Emotional Competencies

Mindfulness	Social-Emotional Learning (SEL)
1. **Singularity** – focus on a single task at hand. The opposite of multitasking. Being fully present and engaged with one thing at a time. Space to learn and hear what our bodies are telling us. **Awareness**.	1. **Self-Awareness** – identify how you are feeling, and how it may be impacting your physical being. Moving learners from powerless to empowered.
2. **Intentionality** – deliberate action moving past tendencies. The opposite of "responding on autopilot" or falling back into the same narrative. This requires disciplined habits of mind. **Ownership**.	2. **Self-Regulation** – ability to respond from a place of calm knowing. Finding responsible and resourceful ways of communicating who you are with those around you. Moving learners from impulsivity to intentionally navigating behavioral choices.
3. **Non-Judgmentalness** – noticing yourself (thoughts, words, deeds) and the world around you without evaluation, appraisal, or assessment. The opposite of "x, y, z was good or bad." **Neutrality.**	3. **Social Awareness** – recognition that our actions impact our classmates, school, community, and ourselves. Moving learners from a reactive, victimized mindset to a proactive, communal view of the world around them.
4. **Space** – Creating mental, emotional, and physical marginality in your life. The space to respond to different personal and social triggers without losing one's center or sacrificing social rapport. The opposite of dysfunctional "groupthink" or habitual, unconscious reactions to everyday events. **Consciousness.**	4. **Balance between Self-Efficacy and Social Harmony** – managing vulnerability with a compassionate understanding of one's relationship with SELF and with others. Moving learners from projection, assumption, or excessive self-sacrifice to feeling centered, present, and like a valued and contributing member of the world around them.

Mindful Practices team, and aligns our SEL competencies with the tenets of mindfulness.

If we view mindfulness as content that must be scaffolded and diversified, just like traditional academic content, then we must look for alternative ways to deliver the content. Traditionally, mindfulness has not always included movement. However, I view the inclusion of movement as a compassionate approach to honor students where they are, realizing that they can find their "center" coming from many angles (Figure 2.1).

As our Mindful Practices model illustrates (SEL + Mindfulness + Yoga), sometimes it is movement, not stillness, which is the most accessible and calming practice for students – especially if those students have experienced trauma or live in a community where trauma is prevalent.

Figure 2.1 Different ways to Get Back to Center

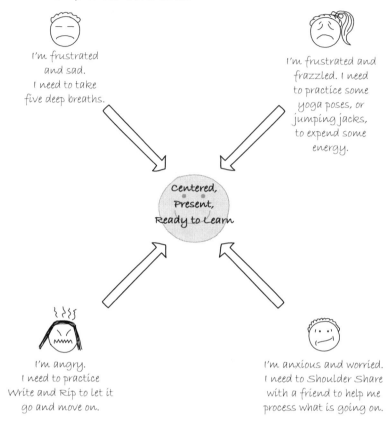

Some students may not have experienced trauma, but are negatively impacted by having too little sleep the night before or too much sugar at lunch earlier that afternoon. Or, they simply have different constitutions, just like adults. My husband likes to go to the gym to work off stress, while I like to curl up with *The New Yorker*. To "relax" on vacation, he wants to snowboard down the triple black bowl with our daredevil friends, while I want to gently glide down the green trail with a hot cocoa in one hand. Whether students or adults, what our bodies crave in states of stress or relaxation varies greatly. Therefore, a practitioner that is compassionate, flexible, and responsive, instead of looking for the quick and easy one-size-fits-all SEL model, will have a much more impactful program.

This variance in student need is why the Mindful Practices model also includes yoga and movement, instead of the standard seated or scripted approach to SEL and mindfulness. If the end goal is for students to be empowered with the tools to move through survival (fight, flight, or freeze) mode when activated, then movement as well as stillness must be included for those learners that find movement more accessible and soothing. It is important that teachers meet students where they are and move their energy accordingly. As my dear friend Lara Veon, who is a trauma therapist and a member of my Mindful Practices team, articulates:

> Because each child's nervous system is unique, what is relaxing to one student might be activating to another. Stillness, for example, might actually activate the sympathetic nervous system – the stress response – instead of inducing a state of balance or relaxation. In these cases, movement with breath work can be helpful alternatives to bring the parasympathetic nervous system – the rest and relaxation response – back online for a child.

★ **Teacher Tip:** As Lara wisely advises the educators she trains, it is imperative that we see all students and their behaviors through a trauma-informed lens. We know trauma is a subjective nervous system reaction to an experience, not the actual event. When we understand the neurobiology of trauma and know that it might show up in the classroom, we can better create environments where students and teachers have the necessary tools for Self-Awareness and Self-Regulation. It is how a person responds to an event that determines if it is traumatic or not, not the actual event. Trauma is in the nervous system, not the event. What is required is an explanation of the neurobiology of trauma and how it shows up in the classroom. It requires us to understand what happens when the body is in a trauma response. Contact Lara at laraveon@gmail.com, if you are interested in more information on trauma-informed practices in schools. Also, the National Child Traumatic Stress Network Schools Committee has a great resource, *Child Trauma Toolkit for Educators* (2008), or check out the Trauma and Learning Policy Initiative's work, *Helping Traumatized Children Learn*, Volume 2 (2013).

When working with different schools across the country, I will often see teachers flip the lights or use shaming language such as, "I don't know what is wrong with this class today. You all are acting like crazy people," in an attempt to corral a high-energy class. While this "shaming" strategy may work for a minute or two, the frenetic energy of the class inevitably resurfaces, as the students were not given the tools or opportunity to self-reflect. As an alternate to using shaming language, I often suggest that teachers move to a mindfulness activity to help students cultivate

Self-Awareness and avoid the retreat to a "fight, flight, or freeze" response that shaming language or triggering situations often brings.

I have included a few sample lessons below to expand on your classroom's mindfulness practices.

Not sure which practice to choose? Do a quick "Thumb Check" or POP Chart Check-In with your students to inform your choice!

Whole-Group Instruction

For a **lethargic class**, honor where they are by beginning with relaxed energy and shifting to activities with more vibrant energy.

> Five-Part Breath (p. 100)
> Shoulder Share (p. 132)

For a **frenetic class**, honor where they are by beginning with dynamic energy and shifting to activities with more centered energy.

> Index Card Scavenger Hunt (p. 124)
> Movement Improv (p. 121)

Individual Student Break

For a **lethargic student**, honor where he is by beginning with relaxed energy and shifting to activities with more vibrant energy.

> Cool Down Breath (p. 108)
> Write and Rip (p. 91)

For a **frenetic student**, honor where he is by beginning with dynamic energy and shifting to activities with more centered energy.

> Standing Yoga Sequence (p. 88)
> Ready to Learn Breath (p. 98)

3

Getting Started:
Thumb Check and POP Chart

Intentionality is key to creating an impactful classroom SEL program. The mindful set-up of the classroom environment is a critical piece in the program's success, as it creates a safe environment in which learning takes place. When done well, the classroom culture is palpable; you can see it, hear it, and feel it as soon as you enter the room.

Below is a quick checklist to help you lay the groundwork before implementation begins with your students:

☑ Did you reflect on your needs as a classroom teacher before setting your classroom SEL or mindfulness routine? What are the times each day/class period when the climate and culture of your classroom is compromised? What negatively impacts your Self-Efficacy and that of your students?

☑ Did you create a Call to Action, such as Being In the Zone or Being the Solution that you can message consistently to your students? Can you implement this with fidelity so that it becomes the lens through which your students view their experience within your walls?

☑ Did you make sure the seating in your room is laid out so that students can feel emotionally, physically, and mentally safe moving their bodies, exploring their breath, engaging in difficult conversations, and working independently?

☑ Did you designate bulletin boards, wipe boards, and wall space in your classroom for your SEL tools (see Chapter 4): a POP Chart, your signed Agreements poster, Boom Board!, Pants on Fire!, and space for supplies including sticky notes, pencils, the POP Box, and a Talking Stick?

☑ What do you need to be consistent and implement with fidelity? Whether you use verbal cues or non-verbal ones, such as dimming the lights or playing music, to move student attention, reflect on which cues work best for you and implement with integrity.

What Does Implementation Look Like?

Starting the School Day with a Thumb Check

To take a cue from one of our terrific partners, Distinctive Schools, I recommend that all school stakeholders check in with students as they enter the building at the start of each school day. For instance, from 7:45am to 7:55am, teachers, administrators, deans, social workers, parent volunteers, custodians, and lunchroom staff are in the hallways with students, greeting them warmly, making eye contact, utilizing the "Thumb Check" (see below), and messaging the school's Call to Action. The school's culture is visceral, real, and rich. For this "all hands on deck" approach to work, the shared value for all school stakeholders is that *nothing* – answering emails, being on the phone with parents, texting a friend, entering grades, or squeezing in that last bit of photocopying – trumps the importance of being present for the students. It is a shared expectation for each and every adult in the building. This also gives school stakeholders a chance to help support students across their school experience. "Hi, Ms. Jimenez. I connected with Taki as he entered school this morning. He mentioned he is having a Thumbs-Down day. Do you mind checking in with him later during your PE class?"

Thumb Check

At multiple points throughout the day, whether it is before school, after school, in the hallway or during their third-period class, a teacher may ask students for a "Thumb Check." The purpose of a Thumb Check is first and foremost to create caring, connecting relationships between students and adults. It is also a practical tool to gauge students' energy, feelings, or emotions. The teacher simply signals the students to hold their thumbs against their chests, which is quick and easy if the class is transitioning between activities, if there is a field trip or a school assembly, or if a student is interacting with a teacher one-on-one.

Thumbs-Up = I'm great!
Thumbs to the Side = Mweh. I'm OK.
Thumbs-Down = I'm having a bad day.

Giving your students multiple methods to "check in" (whether it is via POP Chart or Thumb Check) demonstrates that you are invested in providing opportunities for all your students to practice naming, identifying, and proactively dealing with their emotions. Make sure you review Talking Stick procedures (p. 63) as some of your students may want to share ideas or concerns with the class.

Additionally, encourage all school stakeholders, parents, administrators, staff, and community members to check in with students as part of the morning greeting and at any point over the course of the school day with a quick "Thumb Check." Additionally, empower your "Thumbs-Down Students" to Be the Solution and select an activity from the POP Chart to help positively shift their energy so that they can be attentive and present learners.

Morning POP Chart Check-In (1.5 minutes)

For a more thorough approach to SEL in your classroom, give your students 1.5 minutes of music to get their materials organized and visit the POP (Pause – Own It – and Practice) Chart (Figure 3.1) as they enter class. As the music plays, students PAUSE to check in with how they are feeling. Then, they OWN IT by moving their name magnets to indicate their emotions/feelings. Lastly, they choose an activity to PRACTICE that will help them self-soothe and be present for the class period ahead. Encourage students to add a burning thought, concern, or comment to the Pants on Fire! board or to the POP Box.

Depending on your school's policy on cell phones, iPads, and other screens, I would strongly recommend that you make this 1.5 minutes "screen-free." The goal is for students to unplug, find their breath, and be present.

When the music is over, the students are at their desks with all their materials out and ready to learn.

For those individual students that have moved their magnets to indicate they are having a difficult time, find a time during instruction to connect with that student and offer a SEL or mindfulness practice that would meet their needs. Sometimes, they just might need to connect with an adult. Offer a time to chit-chat before or after school.

It is recommended that the teacher set clear expectations with students, to help ensure that the POP Chart Check-In routine is a smooth, fluid, and

Figure 3.1 POP Chart

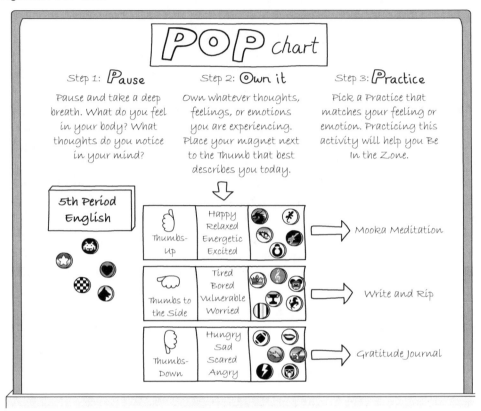

safe process. Whole-class implementation (Tier 1) is preferred, with extended time in the POP Chart for students with exceptionalities or who need assistance modifying their behavior. These additional minutes can be added to the POP Chart Check-In to give students extra processing time. (Or, for advisory periods, extend the time to 2–3 minutes, followed by 5–10 minutes of a guided Talking Stick discussion, Shoulder Share, or Thought Partner Debrief.)

> Like adults, kids have legitimate concerns: hunger, fatigue, fear, a desire to do certain things, a desire for approval, a tendency to avoid things they are not good at, a desire not to be embarrassed or humiliated, and so forth.
>
> Ross Greene (2014)

The goal of embedding SEL and mindfulness into your school day is not to improve your ability to manage your class, (although that is an added perk). The goal of the POP Chart Check-In is to empower students to Pause (breathe), Own it (name their emotions/feelings), and Practice (a solution) so that students are given the tools to deal with the "legitimate concerns" that keep them from learning.

Formal SEL instruction concludes each week with a culturally relevant SEL Story on Fridays. While we have found that 25-minute lessons are ideal for the delivery of SEL instruction, as a former high school teacher, I know that is not possible. So, I have modified that timeframe to meet the needs of the typical 50-minute secondary class schedule. Also, as time is often scarce in our current high-stakes testing environment, this book contains SEL, mindfulness, and yoga lessons that are easily to implement within a timeframe of between 2 and 7 minutes.

Your Classroom SEL practice every **Monday–Thursday**:
POP Chart Check-In as students enter class
+ Activity before test/quiz/group work

Your Classroom SEL practice every **Friday**:
POP Chart Check-In as students enter class
+ Talking Stick (p. 63) discussion or Shoulder Share (p. 132) on happenings of the week

Additionally, the POP Chart activities are there at any time if you need your class to Get In the Zone, or if individual students need a break to relax, energize, or focus.

Anytime a new activity is learned, an index card for that activity should be added to the POP Chart (Figure 3.1). That way, you and the students can have access to the activity when needed. To build student ownership of the POP Chart, encourage them to add activities that they have tried outside of your class to the POP Chart.

If you teach on a block schedule, I would recommend incorporating a SOCIAL SEL activity (see Chapter 8) like Cooperation Circle, Pass the Clap Circle, or Shoulder Share into the last third of your class period, when the class would benefit from a movement break.

The Mindful Practices POP Chart empowers students to Pause and identify what is keeping them from being present and ready to learn. Communication devices, such as Pants on Fire! (p. 67) and Boom Board! (p. 65), along with non-traditional tools like Silent Practice (p. 134), create a way for both students and teachers to give voice to their SEL needs in the context of the classroom setting.

Defining SEL and Establishing Protocols and Procedures

Once the classroom has been set up, it is important to take the time to walk students through their daily routine prior to starting instruction. Model the strategies for the students, demonstrating how to perform a check-in, use an activity in the POP Chart, add a sticky note to the Boom Board!, etc. As Harry Wong points out in his *Facilitator's Handbook* (2009), consistently practiced classroom routines at the start of the school year can be the key to student success. Have activities posted clearly as part of your daily schedule (Figure 3.2). Reinforce an emotionally and physically safe classroom environment by being transparent and consistent.

POP Chart Scenarios for the Classroom Community

Given the importance of a positive and collaborative climate and culture, *these teacher scripts in italic type below* help us utilize the Thumb Check or POP Chart to bring our classroom back together to a centered, present, and compassionate place.

Frenetic Energy

It is the week before Winter Break and the teacher notices her class is unusually frenetic. Instead of using shaming language such as "I cannot believe what a mess you all are today!" the teacher recruits the students' help in finding a solution to set her class up for a successful group work activity.

"OK, ladies and gentlemen, I notice we have a lot of extra energy this morning. Let's Be the Solution and use an SEL activity to be present and focused. [Student name], what activity from our **POP Chart** *do you think could help us get centered?* [Student responds. Teacher or student facilitates activity.] *Great job Fifth Period! Before we transition back to our assignment, I would like to get a quick* **Thumb Check** *from our room.* [Students hold thumbs up to chest, teacher takes a moment to process where the energy of the class is and whether they need another activity or are ready to continue with their assignment.] *Thank you, class. It looks like we are ready to proceed with our group assignment.*

Stressed Students

It is the week before finals. The teacher is starting a review "quiz" in 5 minutes and knows her students would benefit from a bit of yoga or physical movement to let off some extra stress and anxiety. *"Our class has a big review starting in a few minutes. I noticed that most students entered the room and placed their magnet next to 'Mweh' on the* **POP Chart**. *Thank you for openly communicating with me, so I am empowered, as a teacher that cares about you, to*

Figure 3.2 Daily SEL schedule

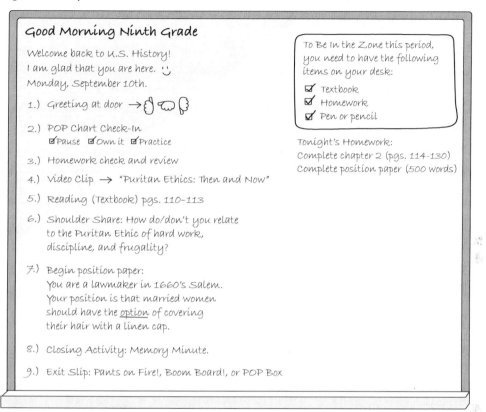

> Good Morning Ninth Grade
>
> Welcome back to U.S. History!
> I am glad that you are here. ☺
> Monday, September 10th.
>
> 1.) Greeting at door →
>
> 2.) POP Chart Check-In
>   ☑ Pause ☑ Own it ☑ Practice
>
> 3.) Homework check and review
>
> 4.) Video Clip → "Puritan Ethics: Then and Now"
>
> 5.) Reading (Textbook) pgs. 110–113
>
> 6.) Shoulder Share: How do/don't you relate
>   to the Puritan Ethic of hard work,
>   discipline, and frugality?
>
> 7.) Begin position paper:
>   You are a lawmaker in 1660's Salem.
>   Your position is that married women
>   should have the option of covering
>   their hair with a linen cap.
>
> 8.) Closing Activity: Memory Minute.
>
> 9.) Exit Slip: Pants on Fire!, Boom Board!, or POP Box
>
> To Be In the Zone this period,
> you need to have the following
> items on your desk:
>
> ☑ Textbook
> ☑ Homework
> ☑ Pen or pencil
>
> Tonight's Homework:
> Complete chapter 2 (pgs. 114–130)
> Complete position paper (500 words)

add a mindfulness activity to our schedule so that we can be present and focused. [Student x], please lead our class through your favorite POP Chart activity so that we can be focused and present for our review."

Lethargic Learners

*"Room [x], I notice our energy is low, and we still have our research projects to work on this hour. Let's Be the Solution and use an SEL activity to energize our bodies and get ready to learn. [Student name], can you name a **POP Chart** activity that will help energize our class and stimulate our brains?* [Student chooses activity. Teacher again reinforces positive behavior by choosing a new student to lead the class through the selected activity.] *Nicely done, [x] Period. Before we transition back to our assignment, I would like to get a quick **Thumb Check** from our room.* [Students hold thumbs up to chest, teacher takes a moment to process where the energy of the class is and whether they need another activity or are ready to continue with their assignment.] *Thank you, class. Now, we are energized and ready to tackle our research projects!"*

POP Chart Procedures for an Individual Student

You can cue a student at any point throughout the day to utilize a POP Chart activity, if she needs to take a moment to relax, focus, and be present. Wherever they may be, honor where students are and move their energy toward the center, on both an individual and group level. On an energetic scale of 1 to 10, with 1 being Lethargic and 10 being Frenetic, 5 would be Cool, Calm, and In the Zone. For a productive learning environment, we need to move both energetic ends of the spectrum toward a focused center of 5.

> *"Sun-Hi, please practice a POP Chart activity for 2 minutes, so you are empowered to cool down and self-regulate. When you have moved your energy closer to a focused 5, you may rejoin your group. If you need more time, please let me know."*

This process empowers the student with the self-awareness needed to self-regulate when she feels powerless or out of control. It is important that the student owns the shift in her energy, not the teacher who casually observes, "OK, fine. It looks like you are relaxed, Sun-Hi. Now you can rejoin your small group."

The same logic applies when your classroom as a group is out of sync. Given the importance of a positive and collaborative climate and culture, bringing the group back together to a place of compassion and Social Harmony is a priority. Post procedures for taking a break next to the POP Chart. Clearly establish your expectations for POP Chart behavior (i.e., Do students raise their hand to ask if they can get out of their seats and walk over to the POP Chart? What is the procedure if more than one student wants to visit the POP Chart at a time? Are there any times, such as during a test, when the POP Chart is closed to visitors?)

Step 1: Sit or stand facing the POP Chart and set the timer for 2 minutes.
[Encourage students to sit with their backs to the class; that way they can disconnect from the room. Students should not feel as if they are being watched and should not be easily able to distract other students.]

Step 2: Choose one activity to practice for the entire 2 minutes.

Step 3: When the timer goes off, stop the activity.

Step 4: Complete your brief Exit Slip.

Step 5: Place your Exit Slip on the teacher's desk and rejoin our class.

★ **Teacher Tip:** Have Exit Slips printed out and placed next to the POP Chart with writing utensils. On each slip is space for the student's name, the date, and the SEL activity chosen. To complete the Exit Slip, the student writes 1–2 sentences on how x activity helped her get focused and centered. Additional Exit Slip questions may include, "Is there anything you want to add to the POP Box today?" or "How can you meet your SEL needs in another classroom that does not have a POP Chart?" Keep the Exit Slips very brief so that students can complete them quickly and rejoin instruction.

4

Setting Up Your Classroom

The components outlined below are invaluable components of your SEL Classroom. Some of these will need their own bulletin board or space in your classroom (Figure 4.1), and others may simply need an index card in the POP Chart, so they are accessible to you or students at any time during instruction. *Teacher cues for each activity are in italic type, for ease of implementation.*

- ☑ The POP Chart (see Chapter 3)
  A practice to ensure students have space to voice and meet their needs
- ☑ The Agreements (Figure 4.2)
  A list of guidelines to explicitly frame expectations around safe space and equity of voice
- ☑ Talking Stick
  A practice to ensure equity of voice during whole-group discussion
- ☑ Thought Partner Debrief
  A practice to ensure equity of voice during partner or small group discussion
- ☑ Boom Board!
  A practice to create space for honoring and celebrating positivity
- ☑ Pants on Fire!
  A practice to create space for honoring needs and proactively speaking concerns

Figure 4.1 The SEL classroom

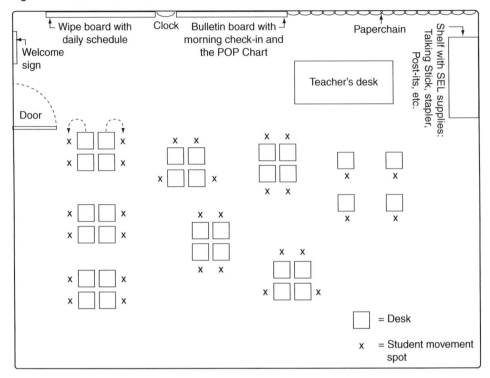

☑ The Agreements

Below are sample Agreements to build consensus among your students. The Agreements are implemented to create an emotionally and physically safe place for communication and to guarantee equity of voice. Once revised, the Agreements should be signed by all class members, laminated, and hung next to the POP Chart (see Figure 4.2).

Supplies: Bulletin board

Provide students with the "Why" of the activity: *Our class uses this list of guidelines to explicitly frame expectations around safe space and equity of voice.*

1. **Be fully present! Check in every morning so you are Ready to Learn.**
    Pause, Own It, and Practice (POP Chart). Learning Posture = sitting up, eyes and bodies toward the speaker. (No hoodies, earbuds, or phones.)

2. **Use our communication tools.**
   Boom Board!, Pants on Fire!, POP Box, and Talking Stick. Find your voice.
3. **Be the Solution.**
   Do your actions help our class be focused and centered? Does your attitude help you think creatively about solutions?
4. **Honor our classroom.**
   Keep it creative, compassionate, kind, equitable, communicative, safe (physically and emotionally), and inclusive!
5. ***Snaps* and Table Taps.**
   Positively witness your peers and hold each other accountable.

★ **Teacher Tip:** *Snaps* = students snap three times in the air when they agree with the student speaking. Table Taps = students drum their fingers on the table if someone breaks the Agreements or says something disrespectful such as "All sophomores are lazy."

Figure 4.2 The SEL wall

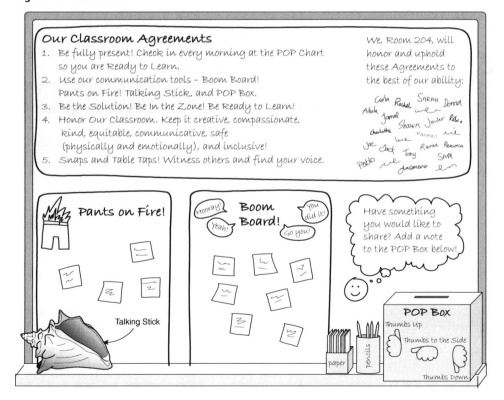

Expanding the Agreements

If you would also like to create Agreements for individual activities, as seen in Write and Rip (p. 91) and Cooperation Circle (p. 116), use the script below to build consensus and safety. Create the Agreements after the directions of the activity have been introduced, but prior to when the activity itself begins.

Before we begin [x activity], I need to find a student who is demonstrating our Be the Solution behavior by sitting up tall, with two feet flat on the floor, and respecting his neighbor's personal space, who can restate our new activity in his own words. [Teacher calls on student demonstrating the expectations. Student restates activity.]

Thank you, [student name]. Room [x], do we see any potential problems with implementing this activity? [Teacher calls on one or two students to discuss potential pitfalls.]

Thank you, [student names]. So, now that we know where the problems may occur, how can we Be the Solution? What Agreements do we need to make for the activity to be physically and emotionally safe for all? What are the consequences if the Agreements are broken?

> ★ **Teacher Tip:** For this consensus-building strategy to be successful, it is imperative that you consistently uphold the Agreements and enforce the consequences. If a class member violates the Agreements, then the consequences must be implemented, or else the students will no longer trust that the classroom environment is safe.

We have time for [x number of] students to share their thoughts. Before we share, let's remember to listen intently to others, accept others' opinions, and be careful not to interrupt our classmates.

[Teacher calls on students and writes the Agreements and consequences on the board. This is also the perfect time for the teacher to suggest modifications to the activity for students with limited physical mobility, students with self-esteem challenges, students who are deaf and hard of hearing, English language learners, and students with exceptionalities.]

Thank you, [student names]. Now that we have our Agreements and consequences on the board, let's Check for Understanding.* Please raise *your right hand in the air. A "high five" hand tells me you understand the activity, our Agreements, and the consequences if the Agreements are broken, and you are all set to begin. Two fingers in the air, or a peace sign, tells me that you have a question or comment that needs to be addressed before we begin. A fist in the air tells me that you are unsure and you are not ready to begin, which is OK. It is important that we have created a physically and emotionally safe classroom environment for our activity to take place.*

[Teacher reads room and responds appropriately to student needs by answering questions, restating activity, building consensus, etc.]

Thank you, Room [x], for sharing your thoughts respectfully and thoughtfully. I witnessed students actively listening to their peers. Well done! Now, let's move on to our activity, [x]!

*Adapted from Doug Lemov's *Teach Like a Champion* (2010)

☑ Talking Stick

Supplies: Index card to add the activity to the POP Chart
A soft object that can be passed from student to student (a stress ball, stuffed animal, or something that is not easy to throw).

Time: 3–5 minutes

Provide students with the "Why" of the activity: *We are practicing Talking Stick to learn how to appropriately express emotions, enhance **peer-to-peer communication**, and increase social awareness. Talking Stick ensures equity of voice during whole-group discussions.*

The basic premise of using a Talking Stick as a communication tool is that the person who is holding the stick gets to speak. Although this is a simple principle, to guarantee that this activity is an emotionally safe experience for students, you must create Agreements for use. These Agreements can extend to general sharing, class meetings, or any other large group discussions.

It is recommended that you laminate your Talking Stick Agreements and place them next to the POP Chart in your classroom. Before the Talking Stick session begins, the teacher should write the start and end time on the board. A typical time frame is 3–5 minutes, but the amount of time may vary depending on topic, time of day, etc. For example, Start: 9:15 am, End: 9:20 am.

While each classroom is different, below are a few essential steps for creating your Talking Stick Agreements:

◆ The person holding the Talking Stick is the only one to speak. Each speaker may share for no longer than 30 seconds. [The teacher should establish a non-verbal sign, such as three snaps in the air, to signify when the speaker's time has concluded.]

◆ The Talking Stick is passed silently from speaker to speaker, in the order in which students raised their hands to share. [The Talking Stick is not to be thrown or simply given to the person closest to the speaker.] The silence between speakers is the perfect time for the class to reflect on what was being shared. It is recommended that each speaker take an easy breath, with eyes closed, to collect his thoughts before speaking.

◆ Describe listening expectations for a Talking Stick session. What does active listening look like and sound like in this setting?

◆ The speaker must wait until two more classmates have spoken before they request to speak again. The speaker understands that there may not be enough time for them to have another turn.

◆ The speaker must use "I" language and talk only about his experiences and opinions. It is important that everyone feels comfortable sharing. A Talking Stick Session is judgment-free. [Also include no piggybacking, or restating someone else's point. This guideline often leads to more original and diverse thinking on an issue.]

◆ Conclude the activity with a whole-group **Thumb Check** (p. 50)

★ **Teacher Tip:** Make the Talking Stick available to students during their morning check-in routine. They may walk in with positive or negative information to process. Giving them a positive outlet to share that information not only reinforces effective communication practices in a social setting, it also gives students the tools to be focused, present, and ready to learn.

Restorative Practices: Facilitate a Talking Stick circle to build community and empower students to build consensus or work out a conflict. Before starting the Talking Stick session, manage students' expectations by posting a start/end time on the board and reviewing the Agreements above. Conclude the circle with a reflection activity, like Goal Setting Postcard (p. 139).

☑ Thought Partner Debrief

Supplies: Index card to add the activity to the POP Chart

Time: 8 minutes

Provide students with the "Why" of the activity: *Thought Partner Debrief is a great way to practice* **active listening, peer-to-peer communication**, *and collaboration. Respectful communication is key to positively and compassionately contributing to our classroom community. Thought Partner Debrief is a practice to ensure equity of voice during partner or small group discussions.*

First: Before they begin sharing, cue the students to "Sit up tall and close your eyes. Take five deep, centering breaths to help you be present and focused."

Then: Arrange the students into pairs. Inform the students who will be going first (i.e., longer/shorter hair, birthday closest/furthest from today, etc.). Ask the students to sit facing their partners. The first student shares his thoughts for 1 minute while the other listens quietly. When the minute is up, the teacher loudly says "Switch" to cue the students that the speaker switches.

Next: After each partner has had a turn to speak, cue the students that they will have 2 minutes to discuss the topic together.

Last: When the 2 minutes are up, ask the partners to share with the pair next to them for a final 2 minutes. To conclude the activity, select a few groups of students to report on one point that they both agreed on, and one point on which they disagreed. Conclude the activity with a whole-group **Thumb Check** (p. 50).

☑ Boom Board!

Supplies: Small wall or bulletin board space with Boom Board! sign
Multicolored sticky notes
Pens and pencils

Time: 3 to 5 minutes

Provide students with the "Why" of the activity: *We are practicing* **Boom Board!** *today to* **celebrate the positive qualities of our classroom community***. Often complimenting our classmates can be difficult, not only because it requires open peer-to-peer communication, but also because we have to* **manage our vulnerabilities***. Boom Board! is a great practice to create space for honoring ourselves and our peers. Boom Board! supplies are available in the [location] so you can add to it as part of our check-in routine or whenever you visit the POP Chart throughout the period.*

Read the directions below aloud while your students follow along. Then, once the practice is established, include Boom Board! as part of your students' check-in routine.

First: *Take a deep breath and think of a reason you are proud of one of your classmates, such as for being a compassionate friend, helping someone in need, or being adaptable in a tough situation.*

Then: *On your sticky note, give that person a Boom! In other words, write a few sentences witnessing that person's strengths, kindness, or accomplishments. Your sentence might sound like: "Boom! to Nelda for helping the foreign exchange student find her classroom this morning," or "Boom! to Luca for solving the case of the missing water bottles during yesterday's field trip to the Arts Center!"*

Next: *Review what you wrote, and breathe in feelings of community, collaboration, teamwork, and pride.*

Last: *Sign and date your sticky note. Place it up on the Boom Board! to celebrate our classroom community.*

★ **Essential Steps and Teacher Tips:**
◆ Close your week by collecting the sticky notes off the Boom Board! and reading three to five notes aloud to the class. If possible, try to vary which students are acknowledged each week.
◆ Remind students that the Boom Board! supplies are always available so that they are able to add to the Boom Board! as part of their morning routine or when they go to the POP Chart throughout the day.
◆ Save the Booms! from week to week in your students' files. During state testing week, place one of those Booms! on each student's desk to help counter the negative self-talk that often arises during testing time.

- Utilize the Boom Board! throughout the school day when you witness students helping one another, being compassionate, or collaborating: "I noticed Fez helping his study partner tackle the essay questions. I am going to add Fez to the Boom Board!" And, most importantly, encourage students to do the same, "Jackson, thank you for sharing that Willie was super-helpful with the study guide. Are you comfortable adding Willie to our Boom Board!"
- Employ Boom Board! throughout the school day when students are having a difficult time discerning between instructional and non-instructional questions. For instance, if a student interrupts your instruction to say, "I love your earrings, Ms. Wong!", instead of addressing the comment and losing the pace of your instruction, you reply, "Thank you, LaRhonda. But that sounds like a comment for our Boom Board!" While it is difficult not to return a compliment to a student, it is important that students learn they cannot interrupt your instruction with a series of non-instructional comments.
- For students with exceptionalities, photocopy a template with a smiley face, a space for students to draw their Boom!, and a line to write their names. Have a sample posted near the Boom Board! for students to reference. This helps make the activity accessible for students with limited writing proficiency.

☑ Pants on Fire!

Supplies: Small wall or bulletin board space with Pants on Fire! sign
Multicolored sticky notes
Pens and pencils

Time: 3 to 5 minutes

Provide students with the "Why" of the activity: *Pants on Fire! helps us communicate urgent, troubling matters that are preventing us from being present, feeling emotionally or physically safe, or being ready to learn. Often, having difficult conversations or bringing up problems can be challenging, not only because it requires open peer-to-peer communication, but also because it requires that we express our emotions and step into vulnerability. Pants on Fire! is an excellent communication tool for creating space to honor our needs and proactively speak concerns.*

Read the directions below aloud while your students follow along. Remind students that supplies for Pants on Fire! are available at any point throughout class.

First: *Take a deep breath and notice what you are feeling in your body. Reflect on the reason you are feeling triggered or activated, such as being upset that something is seemingly unfair, being concerned that something is unsafe, or needing to express a negative emotion you are experiencing.*

Then: *On your sticky note, write a few sentences explaining your concern. Your sentence might sound like, "I am upset that I missed breakfast this morning. I am hungry and I cannot concentrate," or "I am worried about our math test this period because I left my homework at my dad's and couldn't study." Notice, there are only "I" statements on the Pants on Fire! board.*

Next: *Review what you wrote and take a deep breath. Notice how you feel seeing the words on the paper. Notice if there is anything else you need to write to be able to let go, focus, and be present.*

Last: *Sign and date your sticky note and post it to the board. Take a moment to pause and check in. Reflect on how you are feeling after finding your voice and expressing your needs. How can you find your voice at home or outside of the classroom when the Pants on Fire! board is not present? When I have a moment, I will read the sticky notes and will address the situation when I feel the time is right.*

★ **Essential Steps and Teacher Tips:**
- Walk past Pants on Fire! a few times each day to get a sense of what your students are experiencing that they may/may not be able to articulate. Follow up with students on urgent or timely items.
- Remind students that Pants on Fire! is a communication tool. Even though the teacher cares very much, she may not be able to solve every problem that appears on the board.
- File Pants on Fires! from week to week in your students' files. Then, during parent–teacher conferences, you have a reminder of reoccurring themes that may help inform your conversations with parents.
- Utilize Pants on Fire! throughout the school day when students are having a difficult time discerning between instructional and non-instructional questions. For instance, if a student interrupts your

instruction to say: "I don't have a new bus schedule. I need to call my mom and tell her when to pick me up!" Instead of addressing the question and losing the pace of your instruction, you reply, "Arnold, that sounds like a Pants on Fire! to me. When we finish this next problem, you can grab a sticky note and add that to Pants on Fire!" It is important that students learn they cannot interrupt your instruction with non-instructional questions or comments.

◆ For students with exceptionalities, photocopy a template with a frowning face, a space for students to draw their concern, and a line to write their names. Have a sample posted near the Pants on Fire! board for students to reference. This helps make the activity accessible for students with limited writing proficiency.

5

Framing SEL for Your Students

In italic type below are 3 days of scripted lessons for introducing SEL, the morning check-in, the POP Chart, Boom Board!, and other components of your classroom. Taking the time to pre-teach the concepts and create a safe space for learning is essential to the success of any SEL program. Diving immediately into the SEL, mindfulness, and yoga activities, without taking the time to lay the foundation, will potentially leave the students feeling confused and vulnerable. As with the other scripted lessons in this book, it is *not* recommended that you read the script aloud word-for-word, as that would not help develop your competency as a practitioner. Instead, the script is meant to be a reflective guide that provides a solid idea of how the content is framed, paced, and managed. Read the script a few times, take notes, and then make it your own.

For additional tips on how to reinforce the concepts of Personal Space and Safe Touch with your students, please see problem 4 in the Appendix.

Day 1: Defining SEL, POP Chart, and Classroom Practices for Your Students

[To cue students that their SEL time is going to start, the teacher begins the music.]

Room [x], I have started the music. When the song is over, I expect to see learning posture at your desks – eyes and bodies toward me, all screens and headphones put away, and hoodies off. Nicely done. Thank you.

[Teacher stops music, students are in seats ready to begin.]

I am very excited because this week we begin Social-Emotional Learning, or what we call SEL!

Let's begin by breaking down the name Social-Emotional Learning. Please get out a sheet of loose-leaf paper and fold into three sections. Label the first section "Social," the second section "Emotional," and the last section "Learning." Social is interacting with your classmates, friends, family, teachers, and adults in our school community! So, to help us tune into the Social component, you have 30 seconds to write down the names of each and every person you have interacted with in the past 36 hours. Go! [Teacher sets timer for 30 seconds, cues students when time is up.] *Great work!*

Emotional refers to all the feelings and emotions we experience, when we are by ourselves and when we are socializing with others. Like how it is important to be compassionate, or kind to ourselves, so then we can learn to be compassionate or kind to others. To help us connect with the Emotional component, you will have 30 seconds to write down each and every emotion you have experienced in the past 36 hours. Go! [Teacher sets timer for 30 seconds, cues students when time is up.] *Nicely done!*

The last part of the name is Learning: Social-Emotional Learning; learning about our behavior and interactions with others along with our feelings and emotions. But, since this is a school, the word Learning also has a special meaning. Here, Learning can also mean that if our behavior, emotions, and interactions with others are positive, they can help us Be the Solution or be focused and centered. So, for the word Learning, let's pause and reflect for a moment. What do you most want to learn about yourself? Like how to keep your cool in tough situations or how can you be more compassionate with others? You have 30 seconds to write down three things you would like to learn about yourself or your interactions with others. [Teacher sets timer for 30 seconds, cues students when time is up.] *Thanks, good work [x] Period!*

Social-Emotional Learning is the process through which we develop Self-Awareness – being aware of how emotions and feelings affect our bodies and minds and influence how we make decisions. Social-Emotional Learning helps us look at how the consequences of our actions affect our classmates, our school, and ourselves. By studying Social-Emotional Learning, we can self-regulate – or make more positive, kind choices about our behavior – so that we can be compassionate toward others and ourselves.

Social-Emotional Learning helps us understand our emotions so we can calm down, focus, and be Ready to Learn.

*The activities that we learn during our Social-Emotional Learning time will be added to our **POP Chart** so that we can use them personally, or as a group to* *regulate our behavior. School is a place where we need to work on our SELF skills, such as taking a test or managing anger, and our SOCIAL skills, such as working as a team or behaving well when our class has a substitute teacher. You will also notice that some activities may help you energize* [teacher motions to the chart], *while other activities may help you focus. The activities, or strategies, are broken up in this way on the chart so that we can cultivate Self-Awareness and get to know ourselves, or build Social Awareness and learn how our energy and actions impact our classroom community.*

★ **Teacher Tip:** At this point, I would recommend introducing students to the Mindful Practices model (Figure 1.2) so that they begin to understand the progression from basic needs ("fight, flight, or freeze") to the balance between Self-Efficacy and Social Harmony.

The POP on our chart stands for "Pause – Own It – and Practice." This is how we approach our feelings and emotions during our check-in routine each class period. [Teacher walks to center and points to pocket chart.] *Let's take a look at our POP Chart.*

First, you will PAUSE to notice what you are feeling. Then, you OWN what you are feeling, by placing your magnet next to the thumb that best depicts your emotion that day. Last, you will find a PRACTICE that best meets your emotional needs so you can Get In the Zone and be Ready to Learn.

For instance, let's say you are checking in tomorrow morning, after you had a fight with your sister at breakfast. You PAUSE and notice that the emotion you are coming to school with is anger, because you are still upset about the fight. So, you OWN your emotions and place your magnet next to the Thumbs-Down, which communicates to me and your classmates that you are upset. [Teacher demonstrates.]

Next, you will find which activities in the PRACTICE column can help you self-soothe and calm down. Self-soothing is when you take a moment to be kind and compassionate with yourself. When we take a moment to be kind to ourselves, it is easier to let go of anger and be present in the moment.

It is important that you always check in at the **POP Chart** *when you enter class. That way, you have an opportunity to PAUSE and name the emotion you are feeling, instead of carrying it with you all day. By OWNING it you are able to find the right SEL tool to PRACTICE, so that you can cool down, focus, and be Ready to Learn. Our POP Chart Check-In will only take 1.5 minutes. On days when time is tight, or when there is a shortened schedule, I will ask you to give me* a **Thumb Check**, by placing your thumb to your chest up, sideways, or down [teacher demonstrates], so I can get a pulse of where our class is energetically or emotionally for the day, so I can modify our lesson accordingly. If I see you before/ after school or in the hallway during passing periods, I might also do a quick Thumb Check, just to see how you are doing. It is important that you know there is an adult who cares about you and wants to give you the tools to succeed.

Let's review! Moving forward, we will check in every day either using a quick **Thumb Check** or by stopping by the **POP Chart** at the beginning of class. The POP Chart consists of three steps. Step 1 is to **PAUSE** and notice what you are feeling in the body and in the mind. Step 2 is **OWN IT**, whatever you are feeling in the body and in the mind. Put your magnet by the Thumbs-Up, Thumbs-to-the-Side, or Thumbs-Down picture that best describes where you are today. Step 3, **PRACTICE** the activity on the POP Chart that will help you self-soothe, focus, and be Ready to Learn.

Sometimes, I will say that our class needs to "Be the Solution" and we will practice an activity together. At other times, I might ask that you go to the POP Chart on your own to practice an activity, before you rejoin the group. For instance, I might say, "Flannery, I notice you are having a difficult time honoring your neighbor's personal space. Please go to the POP Chart to choose a Practice to help you focus and be present." Then, Flannery will choose an activity that will help her focus and make more positive choices. When Flannery feels she is Ready to Learn, she will rejoin our class.

As I mentioned before, we will be consistently adding new activities to the POP Chart each week. Please feel free to add activities to the POP Chart that you would like to share with our class.

To review, there are three different situations when we can visit the POP Chart to practice strategies.

The first is during our check-in routine, when we all PAUSE to notice what we are feeling, OWN what we are feeling by naming the feeling or emotion, and PRACTICE an activity that can help us relax, self-soothe, and be Ready to Learn.

The second is any time our class needs to Be the Solution, and we do an activity together to focus and find our center.

The third is any time you need to take a moment to regulate your behavior and Be the Solution, you raise your hand and ask to go to the POP Chart.

Let's also take a look at our Boom Board!, Pants on Fire!, Talking Stick, and Agreements. These are tools we will develop throughout the year as we cultivate our SEL classroom climate and culture together.

The POP Chart is always here when you need an individual break to help you cool down and be in control of your emotions. Social-Emotional Learning helps us positively deal with our emotions, both personally and interpersonally, so that we *can always be Ready to Learn. Remember, you can always practice your SEL tools at home too!*

Remember, you are the Solution. You are in charge of your own behavior!

Day 2: Reviewing SEL and POP Chart

[To cue students that their SEL time is going to start, the teacher begins the music.]

Room [x], I have started the music. When the song is over, I expect to see learning posture at your desks – eyes and bodies toward me, all screens and head-phones put away, and hoodies off. Nicely done. Thank you.

[Teacher stops music, students are in seats ready to begin.]

Last week we learned about Social-Emotional Learning or SEL. I am looking for volunteers to tell me what Social-Emotional Learning is and how we can use it in school and at home. [Teacher calls on students demonstrating learning posture. Students restate definition of SEL. Teacher writes keywords on the board.]

Let's take a look at this Social-Emotional Learning diagram. [Teacher draws simple diagram on board; see Figure 1.2.] *Can I have a volunteer to explain the diagram to me? Nicely done, [student name]!*

Nice work, [x] Period. Let's remember that Social-Emotional Learning is the process by which we develop Self-Awareness – how emotions and feelings affect our bodies and minds – and influence how we make decisions. Social-Emotional Learning helps us look at how the consequences of our actions affect our class-mates, our school, and ourselves. By studying Social-Emotional Learning, we can self-regulate – or make more positive, kind choices about our behavior – so that we can be compassionate toward ourselves and others. Social-Emotional Learning helps us understand our emotions so we can calm down, focus, and Be the Solution so we are always present!

Let's take a moment to review our POP Chart Check-In. Step 1 is to PAUSE and notice what you are feeling in the body and in the mind. Step 2 is to OWN It by placing your magnet by the Thumbs-Up/Thumbs-Down that best describes your emotion. Step 3, PRACTICE the activity on the POP Chart that will empower you to be present. Remember, if we don't have time for the POP Chart one morning, I will ask for a quick Thumb Check, asking you all to hold your thumb up, down, or to the side, communicating with me where you are this morning so I can make decisions about our learning through an informed lens.

School is a place where we need to work on our SELF skills, such as when we are stressed about a quiz or worried about a friend, and our SOCIAL skills, such as when are working with others on a project or our class needs to improve our behavior. Some of our activities utilize voice, movement, or team-building to help us Be the Solution, and others are individual breathing or mindfulness activities to help be in the present moment. Each of us is built differently and has different needs. The most important thing is to be aware of our needs so that we can regulate our behavior and make positive choices. The activities, or strategies, are broken up in this way on the POP Chart so that we can choose the activity that is the best fit for us on that particular day.

★ **Teacher Tip:** When your students behave inappropriately, you are encouraged to engage them in a discussion about Being the Solution or whatever Call to Action you are using in your classroom.

After we learn a new Social-Emotional Learning or mindfulness activity, we will write it on an index card and add it to our POP Chart. Practicing these activities as part of our daily check-in routine helps us remember that we are the Solution. We are in charge of our own behavior.

May I have a volunteer to explain how our POP Chart can help us Be In the Zone or Be the Solution? [Teacher chooses one last student to share.] *Thank you [student name], because you did such an excellent job discussing our POP Chart, can you lead us through an SEL activity to close this discussion?* [Student facilitates activity, teacher closes lesson.]

Day 3: Final Review of SEL and POP Chart

[To cue students that their SEL time is going to start, the teacher begins the music.]

Room [x], I have started the music. When the song is over, I expect to see learning posture at your desks – eyes and bodies toward me, all screens and headphones put away, and hoodies off. Nicely done. Thank you.

[Teacher stops music, students are in seats ready to begin.]

These last few weeks we have learned about Social-Emotional Learning or SEL.

If you recall, Social-Emotional Learning is the process through which we develop Self-Awareness – how emotions and feelings affect our bodies and minds – and influence how we make decisions. Social-Emotional Learning helps us look at how the consequences of our actions impact our classmates, our school, and ourselves. By studying Social-Emotional Learning, we can self-regulate – or make more positive, kind choices about our behavior – so that we can be compassionate toward others and ourselves. Social-Emotional Learning helps us understand our emotions so we can calm down, focus, and Be the Solution instead of the problem so we are empowered to be present!

School is a place where we need to cultivate our SELF skills and our SOCIAL skills to be successful learners. You will also notice that some activities help us warm up and energize [teacher motions to the chart], *while other activities help us cool down and focus. Some of us like movement to help us Get In the Zone, and some of us like breathing or relaxation activities to help us Get In the Zone. Each of us is built differently and has different needs. The most important thing is to be aware of our needs so that we can regulate our behavior and make positive choices. Remember, we can always practice our SEL tools at home too, if we are ever feeling stressed, anxious, or worried!*

6

Using the Activities

The SEL activities are broken up into two chapters: SELF and SOCIAL. The activities within each chapter are broken up in the Table of Contents under "Energize" or "Focus." Typically, the energizing activities include more movement and team-building, while the focusing activities include more mindfulness and breath work. Please be mindful that students respond differently to movement and stillness depending on their needs, exposure to trauma, and lifestyle choices.

These practices are designed for whole-class implementation (Tier 1), not for a few "problem students" to implement on their own or only with a social worker. Once the POP Chart is established, the activities become part of your class check-in routine. The teacher may cue students who need help controlling their behavior to visit the POP Chart for a few minutes before returning to class, or the teacher may proactively insert a practice into the school day to help positively shift student energy toward being present. For students with exceptionalities, offer extended time in the POP Chart and include activity modifications to guarantee inclusivity. Guaranteeing an emotionally and physically safe and accessible environment is crucial for program implementation to be inclusive for all.

The activities are either written as "Extended Scripts," which include extensive classroom management cues and pacing suggestions, or are written as "Activities" (often as sequences), to be read aloud by the teacher or implemented as directed.

As I have mentioned in other areas of this book, I am not a fan of scripted material being the main delivery vehicle for practitioners, as it does not build teacher SEL competency or encourage reflection. The intention behind the design of the scripted activities is to give the educator a vehicle in which to learn the delivery, pacing, and classroom management style that best complements the content. Given the length, the scripts are **not** designed to be read aloud to the students. Instead, it is recommended the teacher read through the scripts a few times to get a full picture of what the delivery looks, sounds, and feels like so that an emotionally and physically safe space is created for the instruction to take place. Once the practitioner has mastered the pacing and classroom management cues, the POP Chart becomes a living, functioning element of the teacher's classroom, meeting both student and teacher needs throughout the school day.

The activities are experiential in nature and empower students to read and respond proactively to their bodies' cues. The word "practice" is often used when framing the activities. It is important that the work is messaged to the students as something they practice, instead of something they do once and move on. By practicing the strategies again and again, the students are able to cultivate that duality between the body and the mind. The union between the body and mind is cultivated through four interconnected disciplines:

Vocalization: speaking, chanting, singing
Movement: gross/fine/locomotor, yoga, dance, fitness
Stillness: reflection, mindfulness, breath work, meditation
Team-building: play, collaboration, communication

Most of these elements, such as voice, breath, stillness, and yoga, are interdisciplinary. For instance, stillness can be used to help cultivate an awareness of self while interacting with others, or the personal within the interpersonal. Alternatively, movement can help one find focused energy through a team-building activity. Ultimately, the goal is to utilize a mix of Mindful Practices to build Self-Awareness, Self-Regulation, and Social Awareness so that one can find the balance between Self-Efficacy and Social Harmony: the ability to maintain the needs of the self while in a social situation or, conversely, to balance the needs of the group with the needs of the self.

Using the Agreements and building consensus around the activity is important, not just to build an emotionally and physically safe environment, but also so that the teacher can gain feedback from the students on why they believe they are practicing this skill and what the goal of the activity is. Each lesson contains a cue to "Give the students the 'Why' of the activity" to help build student ownership of the material and to empower them with the SEL knowledge to find their words, name emotions, and be in control of their behavior.

For tips on how to reinforce the concepts of Personal Space and Safe Touch with your students, or additional implementation suggestions, please see Questions from the Field in the Appendix.

7

SELF Activities

Although practiced in a group setting, these SELF activities are designed to engage students as individuals and positively shift their energy toward being present and ready to learn. Please note, each activity is labeled either "Energize" or "Focus," but you may notice that students vary in their needs and responses to different practices.

After each activity has been taught, it should be added to the POP Chart, so that students can utilize it during their check-in routine, if they request a break while in your class, or if you feel your whole class needs a break.

The activities in this chapter are written for high school classrooms, with modifications suggested throughout for students with exceptionalities.

Teacher scripts are written in italic type for ease of implementation. However, to build practitioner competency, I highly suggest reading the activities, taking notes, and reframing them in your own words, being mindful of cultural relevancy and taking the time to see all students through a trauma-informed lens.

Brain Massage

✓ SELF: Energize

Supplies: Index card to add the activity to the POP Chart

Time: 3 minutes

Provide students with the "Why" of the activity: *Today we will be practicing* **Brain Massage** *so that we are empowered to make the connections between* **self-awareness** *and* **body aware-ness**. *I have added a card for Brain Massage to our POP Chart* [teacher points to card]. *That way we can practice this SEL strategy before a test, or any time our class needs help being present. This activity is a positive way to manage stress and anxiety, or if you need to take a break at school or home.*

Brain Massage begins with a facial massage! Close your eyes and take a deep breath. Keeping your eyes closed and your breathing deep, tap your fingertips on your forehead [pause for 5 seconds], *around your eyes* [pause for 5 seconds], *down your cheekbones* [pause for 5 seconds], *on the bridge of your nose* [pause for 5 seconds], *and on your chin* [pause for 5 seconds].

Next, place your fingertips on top of your head and gently squeeze and massage around your head for the count of 10. [Teacher counts aloud to 10.]

Lastly, let's give ourselves a calming temple massage. Place two fingers on your temples. Move your fingers in circles for the count of 10 deep, relaxing breaths. [Teacher counts aloud to 10.]

Well done, Room [x]! Brain Massage is an important Social-Emotional Learning activity. It helps us remember to take the time to care for both our bodies and our minds!

Seated Yoga Sequence

✓ **SELF: Energize**

Supplies: Index card to add the activity to the POP Chart

Time: 5 minutes [poses may be done in isolation or as a sequence]

Provide students with the "Why" of the activity: *Today we will be practicing a sequence of* **Seated Yoga poses** *so that we are empowered to cultivate* **body awareness, self-compassion**, *and* **active listening** *skills. We will close this sequence with a short* **Observational Breathing** *activity or mini-meditation. Yoga and mindfulness activities help us* **focus on the present moment by clearing our minds so we are able to tune into our bodies**. *These SEL practices cultivate self-awareness and prioritize our self-care by including movement into our sedentary school day.*

I have added a card for Seated Yoga Sequence and Observational Breath to our POP Chart [teacher points to card]. That way we can practice these SEL strategies any time our class needs help managing frenetic energy, or to quieten our bodies and minds.

Yoga connects the body and mind through movement and breathing. Mindfulness helps us be centered and present, even when we are faced with distractions. If you ever feel like you are getting tired or that you are losing the connection to your breath, simply pause for a moment and close your eyes. That is no good or bad way to practice yoga. The most important thing is that you listen to your body's cues. Does anyone have any questions about yoga or mindfulness before we get started? [Teacher responds to student questions.]

Our first pose is **Seated Arm Stretch**. *Hold the pose only as long as you are comfortable. Once you begin to get tired, release the pose and find your breath.*

First: *Sit on the edge of your chair, with your feet flat on the floor. Lift your arms to a "T" position.*

Then: *Raise your arms above your head, and interlace your fingers.*

Next: *Flip your palms to the ceiling, and relax your shoulders, moving them down and away from your ears.*

Last: *Close your eyes, and take five deep, slow yoga breaths. Yoga breathing is when you pull a calm, relaxing breath from deep inside your body. Then slowly lower your arms.*

To transition to Seated Twist, students stay seated at their desks. Inform students that twists can be very good for letting go of any unwanted stress or negativity.

First: *Inhale and lengthen your spine. Close your eyes and take in a deep, slow yoga breath. Take a moment to scan the body and the mind. Notice if there is anything negative of which you would like to let go. With a deep exhalation, release it now.* [Teacher models deep exhalation.]

Then: *Keeping your feet planted firmly on the ground, exhale and rotate your torso to the right side. Have your eyes find a spot over your right shoulder on which to focus your gaze. Take five deep, slow yoga breaths. On the last breath, come back to center.*

Next: *Keeping your feet planted firmly on the ground, inhale and lengthen your spine. Exhale and rotate your torso to the left side. Find a spot over your left shoulder on which to focus. Take five deep, slow yoga breaths. On the last breath, come back to center.*

Last: *Close your eyes, and take five deep, slow yoga breaths. Try to clear your mind of absolutely everything. Simply notice the pattern of the breath moving in and out of your body. Don't try to change the rhythm of the breath, just follow it.*

To transition to Gentle Neck Stretch, students stay seated at their desks. This yoga pose is an excellent solution if you feel stress in the neck or body and want to relax.

First: *Before we begin this last element of the sequence, make sure you are sitting on the edge of your chair, with your feet flat on the floor. Inhale and lengthen your spine. Close your eyes and take in a deep, slow yoga breath.*

Then: *Lengthen your spine and place your left hand on your desk and your right fingertips on your right shoulder.*

Next: *Rotate your right elbow so it is in line with your shoulder. With an inhalation, tilt your left ear toward your left shoulder. Maintain a square and still upper body while you use your right fingertips to apply light pressure on the right shoulder.*

Last: *Focus your gaze over left shoulder. Take five deep, slow yoga breaths. If at any point you feel a pull, release the pose. When you are done, bring yourself back to a neutral position with a tall spine. To complete the same sequence on the left side, place your right hand on your desk and your left fingertips on your left shoulder. Rotate your left elbow so it is in line with your shoulder. With an inhalation, tilt your right ear toward your right shoulder. Maintain a square and still upper body while you use your left fingertips to apply light pressure on the left shoulder.*

*To complete the activity, exhale and roll your shoulders back three times and close your eyes. Pause and take 30 slow, deep, **Observational Breaths**. Notice what you are experiencing in your body and the mind. Can you observe what is happening in your body or mind without shame or judgment? Can you accept where you are in this moment without wanting to be better or different? As you open your eyes, identify three familiar objects – like "shoe, desk, and chair" – before transitioning back to our class.*

Standing Yoga Sequence

✓ SELF: Energize

Supplies: Index card to add the activity to the POP Chart

Time: 5 minutes [poses may be done in isolation or as a sequence]

Provide students with the "Why" of the activity: *Today we will be practicing a sequence of* **Standing Yoga poses** *so that we are empowered to cultivate* **body awareness, self-compassion, and active listening** *skills. We will close this sequence with a short* **Half Circle Meditation**. *Yoga and mindfulness activities help us* **focus on the present moment by clearing our minds so we are able to tune into our bodies**. *These SEL practices cultivate self-awareness and prioritize our self-care by including movement into our sedentary school day.*

I have added a card for Standing Yoga Sequence and Circle Meditation to our POP Chart [teacher points to card]. That way we can practice these SEL strategies any time our class needs help managing frenetic energy, or to quieten our bodies and minds.

Yoga connects the body and mind through movement and breathing. Mindfulness helps us be centered and present, even when we are faced with distractions. If you ever feel like you are getting tired or that you are losing the connection to your breath, simply pause for a moment and close your eyes. There is no good or bad way to practice yoga. The most important thing is that you listen to your body's cues. Does anyone have any questions about yoga or mindfulness before we get started? [Teacher responds to student questions.]

When I say "Begin," please stand up and push in your chairs. [Teacher cues students and they all stand and push in their chairs.] *Please stay behind your desk, at least arms-width apart from your neighbor. It is important to keep our classroom safe by honoring our classmates' personal space.*

Our first pose is **Mountain Pose**. *Hold the pose only as long as you are comfortable. Once you begin to get tired, release the pose and find your breath.*

First: *Plant your right foot onto the ground, and count, "One!" Plant your left foot onto the ground, and count, "Two!" Make sure your feet are parallel like train tracks.*

Then: *Shoot your right arm straight down next to your body, fingers actively pointing down, and count, "Three!" Do the same with your left arm, counting, "Four!"*

Next: *Extend the crown of your head to the ceiling to lengthen your whole spine, roll your shoulders back, and settle your eyes on a focal point, counting, "Five!"*

Last: *Distribute your weight evenly between both feet as you stand tall and proud. Take five slow, deep yoga breaths.*

To transition to Tippy Toes Breath, students stay standing next to their desks.

First: *Stand next to your desk with a tall spine. As you get started, place a hand on your chair to help you balance.*

Then: *Focus your gaze on a point in front of you. Choose a spot that is not moving, such as a floor tile or desk leg.*

Next: *Stand on your tiptoes. Inhaling and staying on your tiptoes, bend your knees to lower yourself about 4 inches as you count to 4, keeping your back tall and upright. Inhaling and staying on your tiptoes, lower yourself 4 more inches as you count to 4. Exhaling and staying on your tiptoes, rise back to standing as you count to 4.*

Last: *Let's hone our concentration skills and practice Tippy Toes Breath again together.*

To transition to Tree Pose, students stay standing next to their desks.

First: *Begin by standing with your feet parallel, no more than hip-width apart. Focus your gaze on a point in front of you.*

Then: *Shift your weight onto your right leg. Lift your left leg, and turn it out to the side while you keep your hips facing forward.*

Next: *Place your left foot above or below your right knee. Please do not put your foot directly on your knee, as it is unhealthy for your knee joint. Use the opposing action of pressing your foot into your leg as the leg presses back into your foot.*

Last: *Lift your arms overhead like the branches of a tree. Repeat on the left side.*

To close the sequence, cue students to take their seats for the Half Circle Meditation. All students are seated so their full body is facing the board, not just eyes. Teacher draws large half circle or arc on board. Underneath the half circle, the teacher writes a positive statement about the class. Such as, "I am smart," "I am compassionate," "I matter," "I am enough," or "I make the world a better place by being in it."

The teacher then cues the students to follow the arc, back and forth, back and forth, with their eyes while repeating the statement silently to themselves.

First: *Moving from left to right, follow the arc of the circle with your eyes, without moving your head.*

Then: *While you continue your eye circles, repeat the following statement to yourselves,* [Teacher reads statement off the board].

Next: *We will continue for another 10 breaths, if your eyes fatigue, simply close your eyes and relax until the activity concludes.*

Last: *Finish your last round of eye circles and close your eyes. Exhale and roll your shoulders back three times. Pause and notice what you are experiencing in your body and the mind. Can you observe what was the most challenging aspect of the activity without shame or judgment? Can you accept where you are in this moment without wanting to be better or different? As you open your eyes, identify three familiar objects – like "shoe, desk, and chair" – before transitioning back to our class.*

Write and Rip

✓ SELF: Energize

Supplies: Index card to add the activity to the POP Chart
Music
Scratch paper
Recycling bin or garbage can
Clock or timer

Time: 5 minutes

Provide students with the "Why" of the activity: *Today we will be practicing* **Write and Rip** *so that we are empowered to* **move through being tired, hungry, fearful, angry, or anxious** *to a present, centered space. Write and Rip gives us a strategy to be personally responsible for how negative emotions impact our learning. To participate in Write and Rip we* **Pause**, **Own** *our self-care needs, and* **Practice** *letting go so that we can be present and ready to learn.*

I have added a card for Write and Rip to our POP Chart [teacher points to card]. *That way we can practice this SEL strategy any time our class needs help understanding how emotions impact our mind and bodies.*

To begin, pause for a moment, close your eyes, and scan your body. Notice if there is any part of your body where you may be holding stress, such as your shoulders or your stomach. Is there something stressful that is making your shoulders tight or your stomach hurt? Is there anything on your mind today that you need to let go of? Like something you are worried about or something that makes you angry?

We're going to practice Write and Rip by writing our negative thoughts and worries on a piece of scratch paper, then ripping them up and tossing them into the recycle bin. You have the length of one song during which to write. You may also draw, if it is easier for you to express your emotions by drawing. [Teacher moves recycling bin to the center of the room.] *By tossing our worries in the trash, we are empowered to let go of stress, be in the present, and manage our emotions. Please be reassured that no one will see what you write, even me. You may write – or draw – in English, Spanish, Polish, or any language in which you feel comfortable expressing yourself. All pages are ripped up and put in the recycle bin.*

Before we begin, I need to find a student with learning posture with eyes and navel toward me, feet on the floor, hoodies and headphones off, and phones put away.

To Check for Understanding, who can restate the activity in her own words? [Teacher calls on student demonstrating the expectations. Student restates activity.]

Thank you, [student name]. Room [x], do we see any potential problems with implementing this activity? [Teacher calls on one or two students to discuss potential pitfalls.]

Thank you, [student names]. So, now that we know where the problems may occur, how can we Be the Solution? What Agreements do we need to add to our existing list [teacher points to the Agreements on bulletin board] *for this activity to be physically and emotionally safe for all? What are the consequences if the Agreements are broken?*

> ★ **Teacher Tip:** For this consensus-building strategy to be successful, it is imperative that you consistently uphold the Agreements. If the Agreements are broken, clear consequences must be enforced to maintain an emotionally and physically safe classroom environment.

We have time for [x number of] students to share their thoughts. Before we share, let's remember to listen intently to others, accept others' opinions, and be careful not to interrupt our classmates.

[Teacher calls on students and writes the Agreements and consequences on the board. This is also the perfect time for the teacher to suggest modifications to the activity for students with limited physical mobility, students with self-esteem challenges, students who are deaf and hard of hearing, English language learners, and students with exceptionalities.]

Thank you, [student names]. Now that we have our additional Agreements and consequences on the board, let's Check for Understanding. Please raise your right hand in the air. A "high five" hand tells me you understand the activity, our Agreements, and the consequences if the Agreements are broken and you are all set to begin. Two fingers in the air, or a peace sign, tells me that you have a question or comment that needs to be addressed before we begin. A fist in the air tells me that you are unsure and you are not ready to begin, which is OK. It is important that we have created a physically and emotionally safe classroom environment for our activity to take place.

[Teacher observes the room and responds appropriately to student needs by answering questions, restating activity, building consensus, etc.]

Thank you, [x]-period class, for sharing your thoughts respectfully and thoughtfully. I witnessed students actively listening to their peers. Nicely done! Now, please get out your pencils and a piece of scratch paper. Once we are done ripping up our papers, I will place the recycle bin behind my desk, so that you are reassured that the contents of the bin will not be tampered with. When I say "Begin" I will turn on the music. You will have the length of one song to write or draw any negative emotions or worries you may have. When the song is over, we will all rip up our papers and toss them in the recycle bin.

[Teacher makes sure every student has scratch paper and a writing utensil. Teacher begins music and the students begin to write. It is recommended that the teacher also participates in the activity to reinforce the fidelity of the implementation, so that the students are reassured that the contents of the bin will not be tampered with. When the song concludes, the teacher stops the music and asks all the students to rip up their pages. Teacher prompts the students row-by-row to walk up to the recycling bin to toss their pages. Once the last row is done, the teacher will rip up her page, place it in the recycle bin, tie the garbage bag at the top, and place it all behind her desk.]

Great job, [x]-period class! I am impressed with your behavioral choices. I witnessed students developing emotional awareness and learning a new way to let go of negative emotions. I witnessed students self-regulating and making positive decisions about their behavior. I also witnessed students honoring the Agreements. Thank you!

That way, our class has another strategy to help us be Ready to Learn any time we need to let go of negative thoughts or feelings. Remember, Room [x], we can also practice Write and Rip at home, any time we feel stress in our bodies or our minds.

We have time for [x number of] students to share their emotions and feelings with a one-word check-in. Again, I am looking for students with learning posture with eyes and navel toward me, feet on the floor, hoodies and headphones off, and phones put away, who can share one word with our class. [Teacher calls on students to share one word such as "Peaceful" or "Centered."]

Gratitude Journal

✓ SELF: Energize

Supplies: Index card to add the activity to the POP Chart

Teacher selects and laminates 20–25 random photos or drawings of people, places, objects, occasions, animals, etc. (Please note: these photos should be indicative of a diverse cohort of cultures, races, lifestyles, and ethnicities. Be intentional as to whether the photos you choose depict negative images – violence during Civil Rights Movement or the tragedies of the Holocaust – while powerful, these images may be triggering for some students.)
Notebook or scratch paper
Pens and pencils
Clock or timer

Time: 10 minutes

Provide students with the "Why" of the activity: *Today we will be creating a* **Gratitude Journal** *so that we can develop the space to be thankful and practice showing* **appreciation, kindness,** *and* **empathy** *to our school community. This SEL practice empowers us to* **acknowledge** *and* **express our emotions** *and to build an* **awareness** *of how others, actions influence us and, in turn,* **how our actions influence others***.*

First: Display the photos around the classroom and ask the students to silently walk around the space observing the photos and noticing what feelings and emotions come up for them. As they circulate around the room, ask them, *"Do you connect with any one photo more than another? Observe what you are experiencing when you look at the different pictures. Try not to judge your reactions, just notice them."*

Then: After the students have had about a minute to circulate around the room looking at the photos, ask them to, *"Close your eyes, or focus your gaze, and take three deep breaths. Notice what you are feeling in your body. Notice what thoughts are in your mind. [Teacher waits while students take three deep breaths.] Think of three things that you are most grateful for in this moment as you silently return to your seats."*

Next: The teacher instructs the students: *"Once you have returned to your seat, you will have 4 minutes to doodle, write, or draw something that expresses the gratitude you are feeling. There is no right or wrong way to express your story of gratitude. You can explain which photo resonated with you and why. You can tell a story from your childhood or* *last soccer match. The only requirement is that your pen is in motion for the entire 4 minutes. Get your pens ready – take a breath – and begin!"* [Teacher sets the timer for 4 minutes and writes "Start Time:" and "Stop Time:" on the board.]

Last: Stop the timer and ask students to put their pens down. Ask the students to take five breaths and examine what they created. Then cue the students to, *"Notice what you are feeling in the body and in the mind. Do you feel any different after you Paused to notice all that you have to be grateful for?"* [Close the activity with a quick Thumb Check (p. 74). Or, if time permits, facilitate a quick Talking Stick discussion (p. 63).]

★ **Teacher Tip:** Think of where you would like your students to store their journals. Perhaps they keep all their drawings in a notebook, folder, or binder? If time permits, you can ask the students to share their drawings with a partner. This is a great way to facilitate active listening and to help students manage vulnerability. There are many ways to extend this activity into a classroom practice. For instance, you can keep a "Gratitude Box" in your room, for you and your students to add to at any point through the semester. You can also make time for your students to write gratitude letters to someone in their lives that has done a lot for them. This activity fuses perfectly with the morning POP Chart Check-In routine and it is also a great solution for students who finish their work early and need a productive way to channel excess energy. Whether it is a drawing, a simple note, or a letter, practicing gratitude is a valuable life-long learning tool.

Still Point

✓ **SELF: Focus**

Supplies: Index card to add the activity to the POP Chart

Time: 2 minutes

Provide students with the "Why" of the activity: *Today, we will be practicing Still Point. This activity is a great way to* **support ourselves in a challenging situation by developing our problem-solving skills and emotional awareness**. *This activity has two parts. The first is to help us find a calm, relaxed state. The second is to create a simple way for us to find that relaxed state, or Still Point, any time we are stressed, worried, or need to find our center.*

First: *We are going to find a cooling, relaxing breath by curling our tongues and sipping air through them, like a straw. Let's all inhale now to the count of 3* [teacher models inhalation] *and exhale through our noses to the count of 3* [teacher models exhalation].

Then: *We are going to find this cooling breath again. This time, when we are breathing and feeling relaxed, we are going to cross our middle and index fingers together* [teacher demonstrates]. *Let's practice this together, inhaling through our "straw" to the count of 3* [teacher models inhalation] *and exhaling through our noses to the count of 3* [teacher models exhalation]. *Now that we are relaxed, calm, and have found our* **Still Point***, let's cross our fingers* [teacher demonstrates].

Next: *We are going to practice this strategy again. By finding a relaxing state and crossing our fingers, we are training our bodies to find that peaceful, relaxed state – or* **Still Point** *– every time our fingers are crossed.*

Let's practice it again! Inhaling through our "straw" to the count of 3 [teacher models inhalation] *and exhaling through our noses to the count of 3* [teacher models exhalation]. *Now that we are relaxed, calm, and have found our Still Point, let's cross our fingers* [teacher demonstrates].

Last: *I need to find students who are demonstrating our Be the Solution behavior by sitting up tall, with two feet flat on the floor, and respecting their neighbor's personal space, who can share examples of different times they could use this strategy throughout the day. We have time for [x number of] students to share their thoughts. Before we share, let's remember to listen intently to others, accept others' opinions, and be careful not to* *interrupt our classmates.* [Teacher calls on students demonstrating the expectations. Teacher writes examples on board.]

Thank you, [student names]. Room [x], are there any other times, maybe at home, when you are taking a test, during soccer practice, or over the weekend, when this strategy would also be useful? How can you find your Still Point in other tough situations? [Teacher calls on an additional student to write his ideas on the board.]

Thank you, [student name]. So, now that we know when stressful situations may occur, we can Be the Solution and find our Still Points so we can remain cool, relaxed, and focused.

★ **Teacher Tip:** Continue to practice Still Point throughout the day to reinforce and model the concept for your students. Remind students to "find their Still Points" if they encounter a tough problem on a test or find themselves dealing with stress and anxiety at home. This activity is great for state testing, but should be practiced well before then to give the students a solid foundation for implementation.

Ready to Learn Breath

✓ SELF: Focus

Supplies: Index card to add the activity to the POP Chart

Time: 3 minutes

Provide students with the "Why" of the activity: *Today we will be practicing* **Ready to Learn Breath** *so that we are empowered with the* **coping skills to be adaptable***, present, and centered in the face of the myriad distractions of the school environment. Ready to Learn Breath gives us a strategy to be* **personally responsible** *for how negative emotions, thoughts, or feelings impact our learning.*

Ready to Learn Breath is accessible to you in other classes, at home, or any time you need to problem-solve or find a way to focus on the task at hand. I have added a card for Ready to Learn Breath to our POP Chart [teacher points to card].

First: *Close your eyes and focus on your breath. Just follow your breath as it moves in and out. Try not to change the speed or rhythm of your breath. Leave it just as it is. As you continue to breathe, notice if you feel anything in your body. If you do, don't worry about changing it. Just notice what you are feeling and breathe in and breathe out.*

Then: *Listen for a sound far away, perhaps even outside of our classroom. Focus all of your attention on that one sound, tuning everything else out. Breathe it in, and breathe it out for the next five breaths* [teacher softly counts to 5].

Next: *Leave that noise behind and focus your attention on a sound that is closer to you. Perhaps a noise inside our classroom, such as the buzz of a computer or the hum of an overhead light? Listen only to the one sound, nothing else. Breathe it in, and breathe it out for the next five breaths* [teacher softly counts to 5].

Last: *Leave both sounds behind and focus only on the soft, quiet sound of your own breathing. For the next five breaths observe only the sound of your breathing, tune out everything else* [teacher softly counts to 5].

Now clear your mind. Before you open your eyes, check in with how you are feeling. Has your breath changed? What do you need to do to be Ready to Learn for the remainder of our class period … for the remainder of the school day? Before we move on, repeat this statement three times in your mind, "I give myself permission not to be perfect. I matter. I am enough, just how I am." [Teacher repeats statement softly three times.]

Finally, as we close our Ready to Learn Breath today, picture yourself being focused, relaxed, and Ready to Learn. In the next three breaths, open your eyes. Identify three items that look familiar, such as a chair, a pencil, or a book. Once you have found your three items, sit with your hands folded and your eyes on me, your teacher. This formally concludes our Ready to Learn Breath. However, we can decide as a class to use this strategy any time throughout the week when we need help self-regulating, working as a team, or focusing for a test. We will now transition to [x] activity.

Five-Part Breath

✓ SELF: Focus

Supplies: Index card to add the activity to the POP Chart

Time: 3 minutes

Provide students with the "Why" of the activity: *Today we will be practicing* **Five-Part Breath** *so that we are empowered with the* **coping skills to be adaptable** *and present when we are feeling* **confused, upset,** *or that we have lost direction. Five-Part Breath gives us a strategy to be feel in control and* **understand** *that we have* **choice** *– that WE steer the ship – when we are feeling overwhelmed by school, home, or life.*

Teacher begins activity by writing the following quote on the board:

(1) Attract what I expect,
(2) Reflect what I desire,
(3) Become what I respect,
(4) Mirror what I admire.
(5) I am the creative principle in my life. I steer the ship.

(Adapted from a quotation, author unknown)

First: *Begin seated and place your feet flat on the floor, roll your shoulders back, and lengthen your spine.*

Then: *Notice the pattern of your natural breath. Notice the inhalations and the exhalations. Which is longer? Which is deeper? With your next breath, you make your inhalation and exhalation the same length. Let's start with the count of 5. Slowly count to 5 as you inhale. [Teacher slowly counts aloud 1–2–3–4–5.] Now, also count to 5 as you exhale. [Teacher slowly counts aloud 1–2–3–4–5.] The first part of this exercise is to match the length of your inhalation and exhalation.*

Next: *You will match one inhalation with one line from the quotation above. For instance, for my first inhalation and exhalation I will silently say to myself "Attract what I expect." For my second inhalation and exhalation I will silently say to myself, "Reflect what I desire," and so on.*

Last: *Continue breathing this way until you have gone through the quotation twice. Once you are done, pause for a moment and close your eyes. Exhale and roll your* *shoulders back. Pause and notice what you are experiencing in your body and mind. Can you observe what was the most challenging aspect of the activity without shame or judgment? Can you accept where you are in this moment without wanting to be better or different? As you open your eyes, identify three familiar objects – like "shoe, desk, and chair" – before transitioning back to our class.*

★ **Teacher Tip:** If time permits, close the activity with a quick Talking Stick discussion (p. 63). Encourage students to share their experiences in the activity. Which statement felt the most authentic to them? Which statement felt fake or unauthentic? What did they learn about themselves that can help them "Own" challenging situations and move out of feeling "powerless" or "victimized?" What does it mean to "be the creative principle" in one's own life?

Mooka Meditation

✓ SELF: Focus

Supplies: Index card to add the activity to the POP Chart
4×6 index card or a piece of scratch paper torn in half
Pens
Clock or timer

Time: 7 minutes

Provide students with the "Why" of the activity: *Today we will be practicing* **Mooka Meditation** *so that we are empowered to be* **compassionate and kind to ourselves***, just as we are compassionate and kind to others. Mooka Meditation gives us the tools to manage vulnerability and cultivate positive relationships with our peers and ourselves.*

First: Give students one small 4×6 index card and ask them to get out a pen (no pencils). Before they begin, ask the students to sit on the edge of their chairs with their feet flat on the floor either closing their eyes or picking a spot close to them on which to focus their gaze. Before beginning, ask the students to clear their minds and take 10 deep breaths, focusing on the rhythm of the inhalation and exhalation.

Then: Inform the students that they will engage in a drawing practice called "Mooka." A Mooka drawing is created very slowly without the artist lifting the pen. Mookas can be a circular, square, or repeating pattern. In this instance, inform the students that their Mooka will be made up of one continuous line that does not intersect. (Students will start drawing slowly in one corner of their index card – their drawing will look like one long, winding, squiggly line.) *To be successful, we must draw slowly, mindfully, and must* **accept our mistakes** (students are not allowed a new index card if they "mess up" and are also not allowed write in pencil or erasable pen).

Next: The students will silently draw a Mooka while the teacher slowly reads the Self-Compassion meditation below. After each line, the teacher should take audible breaths, and encourage the students to also breathe.

Self-Compassion is being kind and gentle to yourself, even when you make mistakes.

You are human. You mess up.

You are human. You make mistakes.

I am human. I make mistakes.

We are all human. We all make mistakes.

Take responsibility. Don't make any excuses.

Accept yourself as human.

What type of words do you say to yourself when you make mistakes? Are you unkind or do you "beat yourself up?"

How can you be compassionate and kind with yourself? How can you treat yourself with generosity and respect?

Take three deep, full body breaths and let go of any self-criticism, self-hate, or self-doubt. It is not serving you. Now, let it go. [Teacher pauses here, models three deep, slow breaths.]

Accept yourself as human.

[Teacher slows down even more here. Says these lines with heart and gusto.]

You are important. You matter. You make a difference.

You are important. You matter. You make a difference.

You are important. You matter. You make a difference.

Believe in yourself.

Believe in yourself.

Believe in yourself.

Celebrate all that you are: your successes, your challenges. You are unique.

You are important. You matter. You make a difference.

Last: Ask the students to put their pens down. Just as they began, cue the students to sit on the edge of their chairs with their feet flat on the floor, either closing their eyes or picking a spot close to them on which to focus their gaze. Ask the students to take 10 deep breaths, focusing on the rhythm of the inhalation and exhalation.

★ **Teacher Tip:** If time permits, instruct the students to share their drawings with a partner. This is a great way to facilitate peer-to-peer communication and to help students manage vulnerability. Additionally, think of where you would like your students to store their drawings. The students can keep all their drawings in a notebook, folder, or binder to inform their SEL growth.

Owning My Story Journal

✓ SELF: Focus

Supplies: Index card to add the activity to the POP Chart
Notebook or scratch paper
Pens and pencils
Clock or timer

Time: 5 minutes

Provide students with the "Why" of the activity: *The author Brene Brown wrote: "Owning our story and loving ourselves through that process is the bravest thing we will ever do" (2010). Today, we are practicing the **Owning My Story Journal** to help us learn to be compassionate with ourselves and **bravely accept our strengths as well as our challenges**. As we create our stories, it is important to remember that these stories do not define us, they simply help us own the experiences that make us who we are. For instance, if Ruthie fails a math test, it does not mean she is a failure. Ruthie's story is what she learned from failing the math test. Failing is a step in learning. As Albert Einstein said, "You never fail until you stop trying."*

[Reflecting on the happenings of her class the past week, the teacher chooses a list of five to seven topics and writes prompt on board.] Today, I am telling my story of _____.

Trusting my gut
Failing
Being grateful
Being happy
Being the Solution
Teamwork
Grief or loss
Being kind and compassionate to myself
Being kind and compassionate to others
Feeling misunderstood
Forgiveness
Humility
Heartbreak
Being vulnerable
Managing anger

Winning gracefully
Losing gracefully
Keeping my cool in a tough situation
Being strong
Trying my best
Being creative
Taking a risk
Being fair
Following through
Being honest
Oversharing
Keeping my word
Being enough
Communicating
Finding my voice
Listening to my body
Letting go
Doing the right thing

First: Ask the students to take 1 second of silent reflection before beginning by folding their papers in half. Students will have 1 minute to jot down key words and ideas for their story on the top half of their paper. Students may opt to create a storyboard instead.

Then: On the bottom half of their papers, students will have 5 minutes to tell their story. They can write, draw, or create a cartoon. Encourage students to write in their native language.

Next: Once their stories are complete, students will take five deep breaths and read over their story. At this point, they may choose to make edits to their stories, drawings, or cartoons.

Last: On the back of their papers, ask students to write out and sign the sentence below:

I give myself permission not to be perfect. The most important thing I can do each day is try my best.

Signed _____ Date_____

★ **Teacher Tip:** If your school has a relationship with a neighboring middle school or a younger class, facilitating an experience for your students to share their stories is a great way to help them manage vulnerability, engage in community-building, and demonstrate leadership. (What positive modeling for the younger students!) Additionally, think of where you would like your students to store their stories and drawings. The students can keep them all in a notebook, folder, or binder. Or, perhaps share their stories with parents and caregivers during parent–teacher conferences.

Cool Down Breath

✓ SELF: Focus

Supplies: Index card to add the activity to the POP Chart
Everyday object (pen, pencil, key, or watch; no phones)
Clock or timer

Time: 2 minutes

Provide students with the "Why" of the activity: *Today, we will be practicing **Cool Down Breath**. This activity is a great way to support ourselves in a challenging situation by managing our emotions and prioritizing self-care. We can practice this SEL strategy at home, at school, or any time we are stressed or worried. All we need is an everyday object, such as a pencil, eraser, or key, to place in our hand.*

First: *We are going to find a small object, such as a pen, pencil, key, or watch, and place it in the palm of our hand* [teacher models].

Then: *We are going to find a cooling, relaxing breath by curling our tongues and sipping air through them, like a straw. Let's all inhale now to the count of 3* [teacher models inhalation] *and exhale through our noses to the count of 3* [teacher models exhalation].

Next: *We are going to breathe easily and close our eyes. Without moving the object in our hands, we are simply going to notice what we feel. Notice if the object feels heavy or light. Notice if the object feels rough or smooth. For the next minute of mindfulness, we are simply going to breathe in and out, focusing on the feeling of the object in our hands. If our minds wander to other thoughts, let's gently guide it back to the feeling of the object. I will start the timer. Our minute begins now* [teacher starts and stops timer]. *Nicely done, Room [x]!*

Last: *I am looking for three students who can share examples of different times they could use this strategy throughout the day, at school or at home. How can we use this strategy to help us make a positive choice in a tough situation or release stress when we are taking a test? Before we share, let's remember to listen intently to our peers, accept others' opinions, and be careful not to interrupt our classmates.* [Teacher calls on students demonstrating the expectations. Teacher writes examples on board.]

Thank you, [student names]. So, next time we are in a tough or stressful situation, we can use our Cool Down Breath to Be the Solution and remain cool, relaxed, and focused.

★ **Teacher Tip:** Practice Cool Down Breath continually throughout the week. Remind students to "take some Cool Down Breaths" if they encounter a difficult situation. This activity is great for state testing week, but should be practiced well before then to give students a solid foundation for implementation. To supplement the activity, bring textured objects from home or ask students to bring objects found in nature.

Memory Minute

✓ **SELF: Focus**

Supplies: Index card to add the activity to the POP Chart
Clock or timer

Time: 2 minutes

Provide students with the "Why" of the activity: *Today, we will be practicing **Memory Minute** to help us **focus** when we are taking a test or having a difficult time remembering information. Memory Minute is a mindfulness activity that helps us **let go of stress** and **manage anxiety** so that we are empowered to be **present** and ready to learn. We can practice this SEL strategy in another class, at home, or any time we need to be present in the moment.*

First: Make sure your room is quiet and that all screens are turned off or not visible. (Students should not have headphones, phones, etc.) Cue the students to roll their shoulders back three times, respecting their neighbor's personal space.

Then: Instruct the students to visualize a blank sheet of paper and to clear their minds of all thoughts.

Next: Set the timer for 1 minute, and instruct the students to remain quiet. Tap a chime or softly clap twice to signal the beginning of Memory Minute. For 1 minute everyone, including the teacher, is quiet and focused.

Last: At the end of the minute, tap a chime or softly clap twice to signal the ending of Memory Minute.

Expansion Project: Screen Detox

✓ **SELF: Focus**

Supplies: To be determined based upon project chosen

Estimated project time: 3–4 weeks

Supplies: Index card to add Screen Detox to the POP Chart
A few sheets of loose-leaf paper
Pen or pencil

This activity should begin on a Monday. It is strongly advised that the teacher participate in this activity with his students. (The teacher should obtain administrative approval and include a note home to parents prior to introducing the activity to the class.)

Estimated project time: 1 week: 10 minutes Monday (introduce activity), 3 minutes Tuesday–Friday (check-in with participants), and 20 minutes the following Monday (to share findings with a Thought Partner and write a brief in-class essay on the overall experience).

Provide students with the "Why" of the activity: *For the next week our class will practice a Screen Detox. This activity is a great way to* **support ourselves in a challenging situation** *and to* **find the strength to persevere, practice honesty, be disciplined, be accountable to our classroom community**. *This is a mindfulness activity because it empowers us to be present with our emotions, without getting swept into action. The process of checking and rechecking our devices has become second nature to many of us. By being in constant connection with technology, we become caught up in the next distraction and lose connection with ourselves and others. By "detoxing from screens" we are rewiring our brains and bodies to "plug into" the world around us.*

Beginning tomorrow, Tuesday, we will be "screens-free" (no phones, iPads, computers, etc.) for 1 hour between the hours of 7:00 am and 10:00 pm. On Wednesday, we will be screens-free for 2 hours. On Thursday, we will be screens-free for 3 hours. On Friday, we will be screens-free for 4 hours. And finally over the weekend, we will be screens-free for a full 5 hours. Remember, all of our "screens-free" hours must be clocked between 7:00 am and 10:00 pm.

*If you use your screen, or someone else's, for **whatever reason**, you must restart the clock. You must plan ahead; if teachers require you to use screens, you cannot pause/restart your time. You also cannot use this activity as an excuse to get out of schoolwork, home obligations, etc. You must be responsible and accountable in balancing life's demands with the constraints of this process.*

As part of the process, we will be recording our observations in a Witness – Watch – Wait log to share with our Thought Partners next week.

First: *To create our Witness – Watch – Wait logs, please get out a sheet of loose-leaf paper and write your name and class period at the top. Next fold your paper in half the long-way. Then fold it in half again, creating four sections in total* [teacher models].

Then: *We are going to label each section or column* [teacher moves to the board to demonstrate]. *The first column is "Date and Time," the second column is "Witness," the third column is "Watch," and the fourth column is "Wait." Each time we start the clock, or anytime during our "Detox hours," when we feel the urge to look at our devices, we pause, take a breath, and write in our log.*

As your teacher, I will also be participating in the Screen Detox, so I will use myself as an example to review the activity one more time before we begin tomorrow. Let's say my 1 hour Screen Detox is from 8:00–9:00pm tomorrow. Under the "Time" column in my journal I will write Tuesday, February 20 8:00–9:00pm [teacher writes on board]. *In the "Witness" column I will write whatever is going on with me when the Detox begins, like "anxious," "annoyed," or "inconvenienced." In the "Watch" column, I will watch what is happening in my body and mind after deep breaths, "Pausing to take deep breaths helped me objectively acknowledge my anxiety. Writing down my feelings helped them dissipate." Or "Still super-annoyed a minute later. Only got through two deep breaths, instead of three." Finally, in the "Wait" column I will record any additional times, during my Tuesday Detox from 8:00–9:00pm, when feelings came up, "8:30: Wanted to grab my phone, just to check one message. Practiced three deep breaths and waited for feeling to pass." Or "8:45: Got really into reading this magazine, surprised that I didn't think about my phone until now."*

Last: *During class next Monday, we will take 20 minutes to share our findings with a Thought Partner and write a short in-class essay on our experience titled, "Witnessing, Watching, and Waiting: What I Learned from Being Screens-Free." Your completed log, plus in-class essay will be worth [x] number of points toward your final grade.* [If applicable, the teacher should distribute a grading rubric or checklist for the in-class essay, so that expectations are consistent and clear.] *Please note, you will be graded on the* *time and energy you put into the logs, essay, etc. As your teacher, I am much more concerned with the effort you put in to developing self-awareness than whether or not you were a "success" at mastering being screens-free.*

Before we move on, let's practice a quick Check for Understanding. May I have a student volunteer who can share with me what activity we are beginning, when it starts, what breathing activity we can practice if we hit an obstacle, when the activity is over, and how we are graded? [Teacher calls on a student demonstrating learning posture. Teacher writes key words and dates on board, to make sure everyone is on the same page.]

Thank you, [student name]. Remember [x]-period class, there are many other times, maybe at home or when you are taking a test, when the Witness – Watch – Wait log could be useful. As we move through this activity in the next week, reflect on how you can be present and "witness" tough situations.

★ **Teacher Tip:** Continue to utilize the Witness – Watch – Wait logs throughout the year to reinforce and model this mindfulness practice for your students. Objectively recording what we "witness" is a great way to cultivate Self-Awareness at school and at home and is great for state testing weeks when anxiety can be high.

8

SOCIAL Activities

Although practiced in a group setting, these SOCIAL activities are designed to engage students as individuals and positively shift their energy toward being present and ready to learn. Please note, each activity is labeled either "Energize" or "Focus," but you may notice that students vary in their needs and responses to different practices.

After each activity has been taught, it should be added to the POP Chart, so that students can utilize it during their check-in routine, if they request a break while in your class, or if you feel your whole class needs a break.

The activities in this chapter are written for high school classrooms, with modifications suggested throughout for students with exceptionalities.

Teacher scripts are written in italic type, for ease of use. However, to build practitioner competency, I highly suggest reading the activities, taking notes, and reframing them in your own words, being mindful of cultural relevancy and taking the time to see all students through a trauma-informed lens.

Cooperation Circle

✓ SOCIAL: Energize

Supplies: Index card to add the activity to the POP Chart
Music

Time: 10 minutes

Provide students with the "Why" of the activity: *Cooperation Circle helps us* to develop our *leadership, collaboration, decision-making,* and *community-building skills*. *Additionally, this activity also helps us to become aware of our ability to positively influence others in a group setting.*

Cooperation Circle teaches us how to positively interact with others and work as a team toward a common goal. To practice Cooperation Circle, you are going to organize your-selves in a circle according to the month and day of your birthday – **without talking**. *When I say "Begin" I will turn on the music, and you will have the length of one song to silently accomplish this task. That's right, [x]-period class, you* **cannot talk***, at all, while you are organizing yourselves in a circle!*

> ★ **Teacher Tip:** If you are comfortable, give your students permission to move desks or chairs as needed to form their circle. Students will quickly figure out that they will need to use their fingers to cue their birthdays. For instance, if Carl's birthday is February 5, he will hold up two fingers for the month of February. Once he has found his approximate location in the circle, he will hold up five fingers to indicate February 5. For birthdays later in the month, students can stomp once for 10, twice for 20, etc. So, if Maggie's birthday is February 25 she will stomp twice and then hold up five fingers. If you are working with English language learners or students with exceptionalities, please demonstrate before the activity begins.

Before we begin, I need to find a student who can restate the activity in his own words. [Teacher calls on student demonstrating the expectations. Student restates activity.]

Thank you, [student name]. [x]-period class, do we see any potential problems with implementing this activity? [Teacher calls on one or two students to discuss potential pitfalls.]

Thank you, [student names]. So, now that we know where the problems may occur, how can we Be the Solution? What Agreements do we need to make for the activity to be physically and emotionally safe for all? What are the consequences if the Agreements are broken?

★ **Teacher Tip:** For this consensus-building strategy to be successful, it is imperative you consistently uphold the Agreements and enforce the consequences. If class members violate the Agreements, then the consequences must be implemented, or else the students will no longer trust that the classroom environment is safe.

We have time for [x number of] students to share their thoughts. Before we share, let's remember to listen intently to others, accept others' opinions, and be careful not to interrupt our classmates.

[Teacher calls on students and writes the Agreements and consequences on the board. This is also the perfect time for the teacher to suggest modifications to the activity for students with limited physical mobility, students with self-esteem challenges, students who are deaf and hard of hearing, English language learners, or students with exceptionalities.]

Thank you, [student names]. Now that we have our Agreements and consequences on the board, let's Check for Understanding. Please raise your right hand in the air. A "high five" hand tells me you understand the activity, our Agreements, the consequences if the Agreements are broken, and you are all set to begin. Two fingers in the air, or a peace sign, tells me that you have a question or comment that needs to be addressed before we begin. A fist in the air tells me that you are unsure and you are not ready to begin, which is OK. It is important that we have created a physically and emotionally safe classroom environment for our activity to take place.

[Teacher observes room and responds appropriately to student needs by answering questions, restating activity, building consensus, etc.]

Thank you, [x]-period class, for sharing your thoughts respectfully and thoughtfully. I witnessed students actively listening to their peers and Being the Solution. Well done! Now, let's get ready to start our SEL activity for today, Cooperation Circle! Because this activity is non-verbal, let's practice our non-verbal communication skills and making safe, non-threatening eye contact.

When I say "Begin," I will start the music and you will stand up and form your circle. Remember, at the end of the song, your Cooperation Circle must be complete. [Teacher cues the students. Students stand up and form their circle. The teacher **does not** intervene or help the students meet the goal. The teacher's responsibilities are only to be timekeeper by starting and stopping the music and to maintain a safe space by making sure that the Agreements are being upheld. If the students do not meet their goal in time, the teacher can restart the music. This is also a great time for the teacher to positively reinforce the Call to Action and recognize students Being the Solution.]

Well done, Room [x]. I am impressed with your behavioral choices. I witnessed students working as a team. I witnessed students using appropriate non-verbal communication and eye contact. And I witnessed students honoring our Agreements and Being the Solution. Thank you!

There are many ways we can organize ourselves into a circle for this activity. Today, we practiced organizing ourselves by birthday. Next time, we can practice organizing alphabetically by first or last names, or numerically by shoe size, or by the answers to challenging math problems. [Student name], you emerged as a leader in this activity. When the group was floundering, you did a great job of helping students work together as a team. Can you share your experience in this activity with the class? Is there another student who can discuss how any activity like this helps us with peer-to-peer communication or working collaboratively in a group?

> ★ **Teacher Tip:** A fun variation is to have students create other physical shapes such as a peace sign, square, or two concentric circles. For students with exceptionalities or others for whom eye contact is uncomfortable, include the option to write birthdays on scratch paper.

Pass the Clap Circle*

✓ **SOCIAL: Energize**

Supplies: Index card to add the activity to the POP Chart

Time: 7 minutes

Provide students with the "Why" of the activity: *Today, we are practicing* **Pass the Clap Circle** *to give us an opportunity to* **focus, collaborate, and work as a team**. *Additionally, this activity also helps us stay healthy by getting us up and out of our seats to take a movement break.*

First: Arrange your students in one large circle, about arms-width apart, respecting other students' personal space. Before beginning, invite all students to sit (or stand) with tall backs, eyes closed. Ask the students to take a minute of mindfulness by pausing to follow the rhythm of their breath, just checking in with where they are in space and time. Ask the students, *"What do you feel in your bodies? What thoughts are popping into your mind? Try not to operate from a place of judgment, simply observe."*

Then: When the 30 seconds have concluded, choose a student to be Circle Captain and ask him to begin the activity by turning to the student to his left, making eye contact and clapping at the same time.

Next: The student who received the clap now turns to the student on his left, makes eye contact, and claps. This continues until each student in the circle is contributing. The clap moves quickly around the circle, with all eyes following the clap.

Last: After the clap has successfully made it around the circle once, then the Circle Captain should add two more claps to the circle. [It is best if these claps are spaced equidistant around the circle.] Once all three claps have made their way around the circle three times, then the Circle Captain closes the circle with "1–2–3–Stop." [To increase the challenge, the Circle Captain can yell "Reverse!" or "Double Time!" to switch the direction of the claps or increase the speed.]

★ **Teacher Tip:** Modify this activity to learn students' names at the beginning of the school year by moving around the circle saying the name of the student that receives the clap. For instance, the student on my right passes me the clap, so the whole group says "Violet." Then, I pass the clap to the student on my left and the whole group says "Dottie," then on to "Remy," etc. This is a fantastic way to not only learn students' names but also to learn how to pronounce them correctly. For students with exceptionalities, those who find eye contact inaccessible, or those with limited physical mobility, begin by passing a soft, light, and large object, such as a beach ball.

* Adapted from Viola Spolin's *Theater Games for the Classroom* (1986).

Movement Improv

✓ SOCIAL: Energize

Supplies: Instrumental music (no vocals). Soft and slow to start, increasing in tempo when transitioning to the group portion of the activity.

Time: 7 minutes

Provide students with the "Why" of the activity: *Today we will be practicing **Improv: Solo and Assembly** so that we are empowered to cultivate **body awareness** and **engage in self-inquiry** alongside our classmates using movement, **Personal Space, Safe Touch, influence with self and others**. I have added a card for Improv to our POP Chart [teacher points to card]. That way we can practice this SEL strategy any time our class needs an energetic boost or to get back into connection. This activity is a positive way to manage frenetic energy, or if you need to take a break at school or home.*

Every 15 seconds, I will give you a cue to move a certain way. You will move or change shape without talking, even if you are cued to move with a partner at some point. The entire activity is non-verbal. This is a very important part of the process, as it empowers us to be more reflective and tune into our other senses. This activity also helps us stay healthy by getting us up and out of our seats to take a movement break.

For this activity to be safe, please honor the needs of your body. If I say "jump up and down" and your body is saying "I would just rather stand on my tippy toes" then just stand on your tippy toes. The most important element of this activity is to respect and listen to your body. To make sure we maintain an emotionally, physically, and mentally safe space for learning, let me outline the Agreements for this activity:

Teacher reviews the Agreements for today's activity:

◆ Non-verbal.
◆ No headphones, screens, or other distractions that pull us out of connection with others.
◆ Participate with Integrity, trying your best (making modifications, if needed).
◆ Honor others' Personal Space and use Safe Touch.
◆ Honor your body and where you are today.
◆ Be compassionate with self and others. This is a safe, No Judgment Zone – Take a breath, relax, and have fun! (If anyone giggles or coughs during the activity, we will just move past it. We will try our best to only express ourselves through moving our bodies.)

To begin, ask students to walk around the room filling empty space (any space that is not currently occupied by bodies or objects). The students have the option of focusing their gaze to the floor at the beginning of the activity. Slowly, as the students "warm-up," they can begin to make eye contact with their peers – practicing non-judgment. Remind the students to respect their classmates' personal space as they move around the room. This activity is non-verbal; the students should not talk or touch.

Every 15 seconds, give the following cues (each cue will generate a variety of different responses from the students). Be playful in your delivery – smile and be relaxed.

Increase your speed
Walk on your tippy toes
Relax your shoulders
Relax your mouth and jaw
Move only your arms
Move only your legs
Make yourself taller
Make yourself smaller
Move like you are walking through peanut butter
Move like you are walking through water
Expand the time to every 25 seconds, remind students that this ENTIRE process is non-verbal.
Mirror the movement of another
Three people mirror the movement of a fourth person (*Students stay in this group of four for the remainder of the activity*)
You are zombies
You are playing basketball
You are eating pancakes
You are sitting on a cloud
You are listening to waves
Connect with the student closest to you, sitting back-to-back.

To close, ask the students to *"Find a comfortable place to be still for a moment and find 10 deep yoga breaths. If it is comfortable, close your eyes. If not, simply pick a spot to focus your gaze. Find your breath and be present."*

★ **Teacher Tip:** This is a great time to take a picture of your students as a large group, to add to your "Our Classroom Community" bulletin board. If time permits, close the activity with a quick Talking Stick discussion (p. 63). Encourage students to share their experiences. What was inside/outside of their comfort zones? When were they most tempted to talk? What did they learn about bodies/themselves? To add a verbal component to this activity, try introducing a vocal song, chant, cheer, beat-boxing, rhyme, or something that may be culturally relevant and meaningful to your student population.

Index Card Scavenger Hunt

✓ SOCIAL: Energize

Supplies: Index card to add the activity to the POP Chart
Index cards or construction paper
Two shoeboxes
Pens or pencils
Music

Time: 10 minutes

Provide students with the "Why" of the activity: *Today, we are practicing* **Index Card Scavenger Hunt** *to work on our community-building,* ***peer-to-peer communication, and problem-solving skills as well as to help us manage vulnerability****. This activity also helps us stay healthy by getting us up and out of our seats to take a movement break.*

First: Pass out four index cards (or a piece of construction paper folded and torn into four pieces) to each student.

Then: Before the students begin writing, give them a minute of mindfulness to sit with a tall spine, feet flat on the floor, and their eyes closed. Cue them to *"Think about unique, fun, interesting, and special facts about yourself. What would you like your classmates to know about you?"* Then give the students 4 minutes to write four facts about themselves (one per card). For example, "I love avocados," "My dog has two different colored eyes," or "I have a brother in the Marines."

Next: Once each student has completed their four cards, cue them to stand up and place their cards in one of the shoeboxes at the front of the room. Once each student has added their cards, mix up the cards between the shoeboxes and place one shoebox at the front of the room and one shoebox at the back of the room.

Last: Begin the game by asking the students to stand up, push in their chairs, and stand behind their desks with a writing utensil in hand. The teacher calls the students by table to go to the box, and each student chooses a card and goes back to his seat. When the music starts, the students will have two songs to locate the author of their card. The author signs the back of their card, and then the student takes it back to their desk before they grab another card from one of the shoeboxes. (Students are only allowed to have one card in their hands at a time. This will prevent them from grabbing a handful of cards at once.) At the end of the second song the game freezes, and the student with the highest number of signed author cards at the end of the activity wins the game. (If there is a tie, have the students play *rock-paper-scissors* to decide the winner.)

★ **Essential Steps and Teacher Tips:** Depending on your classroom dynamic, below are some management tips for keeping the activity positive, safe, and fluid:

◆ Review expectations for sharing and "oversharing." Discuss what is appropriate and not appropriate (sexual information, violent acts, drugs, etc.) to share at school. It is not appropriate or acceptable for students to judge others or to make negative comments about the information shared, such as saying, "Ewwww. Gross!" or "You're weird" if a student's card read, "I ate goat meat when I went to Mexico for vacation."

◆ In some cases, there may be more than one student to which an author card applies. For instance, the card "My mom was born in another state," there may be two or three students to which that card applies. Before you begin the game, decide if students may or may not sign a card they did not write, but which could also apply to them.

◆ For large class sizes with limited space, have students work in pairs. Each small group has a "home base" where the partners keep the cards, while one student circulates at a time.

◆ When the game has concluded, select a few students to share some information they learned about their classmates. "I never knew that Montell had three older sisters" or "I found out that Alexi's mother was born in East New York."

◆ Keep all the index cards. They are a great way to get to know your student population.

Compliment Partners

✓ **SOCIAL: Energize**

Supplies: Index card to add the activity to the POP Chart
Clock or timer

Time: 5 minutes

Provide students with the "Why" of the activity: *Compliment Partners is a great way to work on our **community-building, peer-to-peer communication, and self-inquiry skills as well as to help us manage vulnerability**. This activity also helps us stay healthy by getting us up and out of our seats to take a movement break.*

First: Play music and ask your students to move around the room filling negative space (i.e., moving to open areas where no one else is standing). When the music stops, cue the students to find the partner that is closest to them. Ask the students to stand facing their classmate, about arms-width apart.

Then: Announce which student in the pair will go first (longer/shorter hair, birthday closest to today, bigger/smaller shoe size, etc.). That student will compliment her partner by witnessing a time that he was exhibiting a positive SEL social behavior such as being kind, compassionate, caring, a team player, a good listener, or thinking about solutions instead of problems. Then, the partners switch.

Next: Give each partner 45 seconds to share a compliment before the music begins again and the students find new partners. Before the partners separate, cue the students to *"Hug, high five, or fist pound your partners to show respect for what they shared with you today."* Continue the activity for at least two more rounds, time permitting.

Last: To close the activity, ask the students to return silently to their seats. Write "I am _____" on the board. Ask the students to *"Turn one compliment that you received into an 'I am' statement such as 'I am witty' or 'I am compassionate.'"* To close the activity, the students will practice a mini-meditation. For 1 minute, they will breathe in and breathe out their "I am" statement, as if it were on a continuous loop in their minds. Once the students have their "I am" statements, ask them to sit up tall, shoulders rolled back, and eyes closed, and set the timer for 1 minute.

★ **Teacher Tip:** For the compliment sharing component of this activity to be successful, it is important you appropriately frame the activity by discussing the difference between a true, observational compliment and a joke or self-deprecating comment. A true compliment would be "You are a very thoughtful and punctual person because you are always on time when we meet in the morning to walk to the bus." Instead of, "I like that you are on time more now because you used to be lazy and show up late, and that was really annoying because I hated standing there waiting for you."

Drawing Out Loud

✓ SOCIAL: Energize

Supplies: Index card to add the activity to the POP Chart
Card stock, scratch paper, or 4×6 index cards
Pen or pencil
Crayons or colored pencils (optional)

Time: 7 minutes

Provide students with the "Why" of the activity: *Drawing Out Loud empowers us to explore the connections between **social awareness, managing vulnerability, and compassion for ourselves and others**. By drawing together, we not only build relationships with our classroom community, we also build awareness of ourselves within our school environment.*

First: Begin the activity by discussing the concepts of Self-Compassion, Empathy, Self-Worth, and other feelings or emotions from the POP Chart such as Happy, Angry, or Vulnerable. Write keywords on the board.

Ask students to get into groups of four or five. Each student needs a writing utensil and a piece of card stock. The students should each put their names on the back of their papers, so that the papers can be returned to the artist at the end of the activity.

Then: Write a question on the board, such as:

Why do we say "It's OK" after someone hurts us? Why does making him (or her) feel better matter more than the fact that *he (or she)* hurt *us*? Next time someone hurts us, what can we say instead?
What does being compassionate with yourself look, sound, and feel like?
What does being compassionate with others look, sound, and feel like?
Who in your life is it hardest to be compassionate with – yourself, others, etc.? Why?
What does it mean to be grateful?
What five things are you most grateful for? Why?
What does it mean to be happy?
How does where I come from shape who I am and how I operate in the world?
How do neighborhoods create emotional and physical dividing lines between people?
Do you participate in friendships and relationships at the cost of YOU? Or, do you make room for the future friendships and relationships that you deserve?

How do you treat yourself? What do you value? What do you deserve?

Do you agree with the statement, "We teach people how to treat us?" Why or why not?

How do you ask for Personal Space or Safe Touch when someone is not respecting your boundaries?

How do you create boundaries with people that have none of their own?

What does it mean to be the person you want other people to be?

What does "finding your voice" look, sound, and feel like?

What does equity of voice mean to you?

What does it mean to have a strong sense of self-worth?

How can being self-aware improve your ability to self-regulate?

What does the balance between Self-Efficacy and Social Harmony look, sound, and feel like?

Give the students 1 minute to draw their answers to that question. When the minute has concluded, ask the students to pass their papers to the right.

Next: For the next round, students will have 1 minute to add to the drawing that has been passed to them. Encourage students to expand on what is on the page. The point is not to have four or five separate drawings. The goal is for the students to express their own feelings and emotions while witnessing and working with the feelings and emotions of their peers.

Last: Once the papers have been passed four or five times, ask the students to return the drawings to their original artists. If time permits, call on a few volunteers to share a one-word check-in on the activity. What did they observe? How did it feel? What did they learn?

> ★ **Teacher Tip:** To keep the activity emotionally and physically safe, it is important to lay a few ground rules. Ask your students not to put any names or identifying information on the paper. They may use familiar public locations, but their drawings cannot depict any one particular person and cannot single out a particular culture, race, ethnic group, religion, sexual orientation, class, or gender.

Check-In and Pass the Squeeze Circle

✓ SOCIAL: Focus

Supplies: Index card to add the activity to the POP Chart
Clock or timer

Time: 5 minutes

Provide students with the "Why" of the activity: *We are practicing **Pass the Squeeze Circle** to help us **develop body awareness** and an **awareness of ourselves in the context of our classroom environment**. We will begin today's circle with a one-word check-in to celebrate our **classroom community** and recognize the interconnectedness we share. This activity also helps us stay healthy by getting us up and out of our seats to take a movement break.*

First: Arrange your students so that they are standing in one large circle, about arms-width apart, respecting other students' personal space. Before beginning the activities, invite all students to stand with tall backs, eyes closed. Cue the students to look around the room and make eye contact with their classmates. Ask them to *"Notice who is in the room with you and appreciate all that they are. Now, take a breath and remember all the unique and special talents that YOU bring to our class as well."* Reflecting on what they observe in themselves and their classmates, ask the students to *"Take a minute of mindfulness by pausing to follow the rhythm of your breath, checking with where you are in space and time. What do you feel in your bodies? What thoughts are popping to mind?"* [Teacher sets timer for 1 minute.]

Then: Select a student to act as Circle Captain for the activity. She will open and close the **one-word check-in** (which allows the teacher to step in and participate once the directions have been given). Before cueing the students, reflect on class happenings of the week and see the sample themes below. (Did state testing begin this week? Was there a gang shooting in the community? Is your class working hard to pass the Constitution Test?)

Next: Beginning with the Circle Captain, ask the class to say one word that:

Describes what you appreciate about your classmates.
Describes what you appreciate about yourself.
Describes what our classroom community means to you.
Describes what our school community means to you.
Describes how you positively contribute to this class.

Describes something of which you are proud.
Describes an example of teamwork you have seen in this class the past week.
Describes what keeps you from giving up when things get hard.
Describes how you stay motivated when you fail and don't succeed.
Describes how to relax, calm down, and get focused when you are stressed.
Describes something that motivates you.
Describes what Being the Solution means to you.

Once each student has said their word, ask all the students to hold hands.

Beginning with the Circle Captain, a silent squeeze will get passed around the circle. The Captain will squeeze the hand of the person to her right, then that person squeezes the hand of the person to his right, and so on, until the squeeze has made its way all the way around the circle. This activity may be done with eyes open or closed, but it must be silent. Once the squeeze has made its way back to the Circle Captain, she will say "Thank you," which will formally close the circle, and students will return to their seats.

> ★ **Teacher Tip:** If there is awkwardness when asking students to hold hands, simply say, "Left hand up, right hand down." To bring a joyous feel to the circle, have students make eye contact and "Pass a Laugh" instead of a squeeze. Laughter is contagious and can bring joy and happiness to any collaborative setting! If there is not time to have students form a circle, simply have them stand up at their desks to speak.

Shoulder Share*

✓ SOCIAL: Focus

Supplies: Index card to add the activity to the POP Chart
Clock or timer

Time: 10 minutes

Provide students with the "Why" of the activity: *Today, we are practicing* **Shoulder Share to continue to develop our active listening skills, manage vulnerability, and practice compassion for self and others.** *This activity also helps us stay healthy by giving us an opportunity to get up and out of our seats.*

First: Write an SEL prompt on the board that you would like the students to discuss, such as ways in which to manage vulnerability, how to be compassionate with self and others, or ways in which to build community. Play music and ask your students to move around the room, filling open space. When the music stops, cue the students to find a partner that is closest to them. Each student is **standing shoulder-to-shoulder** with a classmate, **facing the opposite direction** (not making eye contact). The teacher announces which student in the pair will go first (longer/shorter hair, birthday closest to today, bigger/smaller shoe size, etc.). That student will be the first speaker to respond to the teacher's prompt.

Then: Give each partner 2 minutes to share her thoughts. When the speaker is sharing, the listener does not speak. She does not offer an opinion or advice, she simply listens to the speaker. Once the 2 minutes concludes, the speaker and listener switch. Once both partners have shared, cue the students to *"Hug, high five, or fist pound your partner to show respect for him and what he shared with you today."* Continue the activity for three more rounds.

Next: On the last round, give each partner 30 seconds to retell their partner's story without judgment, evaluation, or advice. The job of the "reteller" is to act as a mirror and help their partner see and hear his own words. "What I heard you say was …"

Last: Ask the students to return silently to their seats. To close the activity, the students will practice a minute of mindfulness. For 1 minute, they will silently breathe in and breathe out a single sentence related to the prompt, such as "Being a good listener looks like _____," or "Being part of this school community feels like _____," as if it were on a continuous loop in their minds. Ask the students to sit up tall, shoulders rolled back, and eyes closed, and set the timer for 1 minute.

★ **Teacher Tip:** As a great stress management activity prior to test taking, have the students share a worrisome thought or feeling regarding the upcoming test, such as, "I am afraid I am going to fail the writing section" or "I hate math and I know I am going to do a terrible job on the math section!" Instruct each partner to respond by asking a follow-up question such as "What can I do to help you in this situation?" or "What does being compassionate with yourself look like, sound like, and feel like in this situation?"

Restorative Practices: This activity is a great way to repair peer-to-peer communication and manage conflict between two students. Take the time to frame the activity with the Agreements and purpose of the interaction ("We are here to discuss ...") to guarantee safety and equity of voice so that each student feels heard and respected. Conclude the activity with a Goal Setting Postcard (p. 139) to help solidify a positive path for moving forward.

* Adapted from Kripalu Center for Yoga and Health's *Kripalu Yoga in the Schools Curriculum* (2015).

Silent Practice

✓ SOCIAL: Focus

Supplies: Index card to add the activity to the POP Chart
Clock or timer

Time: 5 minutes

Provide students with the "Why" of the activity: *We are learning* **Silent Practice** *today to help us develop* **awareness of our body and mind** *and* **engage in self-inquiry**. *This activity encourages us to minimize distractions and be fully present in our bodies and minds.*

First: Cue the students that for the next 5 minutes your class will operate in complete silence. Papers are passed back, routines are run, everything in silence. Alert the students that if they need to cough or sneeze, they should try to be as silent as possible.

Then: Before you begin, ask the students to pause for a moment and scan their bodies. Ask them, *"What do you need to do to be ready to be silent for the next 5 minutes? Let's Be the Solution! If you need to stand up, stretch, speak to me or the person next to you, please do that now. What will your strategy be if you are tempted to speak or distract others during the activity? Could you doodle or journal for 30 seconds or so to help you regain focus?"*

Next: Alert the students that if someone talks or makes a noise, Silent Practice will conclude and you will need to try again another day.

Last: Write the start and end time on the board. For example, Start: 9:15 am, End: 9:20 am. When you are ready, begin the timer and cue the students that their Silent Practice has begun. To close Silent Practice, ask students to reflect on their experience being present in the activity: *"Where did your minds go? Did you notice the sounds of the room? Were you more present with your classroom community? Did you daydream or did your imaginations wander?"*

★ **Essential Steps and Teacher Tips:**

◆ Start your Silent Practice with small increments of time, like 5 minutes. Then, build up to 15 or 20 minutes by the end of the year.

◆ Do not make this "silent reading time" but instead, use this as an opportunity to nurture students' ability to self-regulate during classroom routines by giving them the space to notice their impulses and how those impulses impact and/or support their classroom community.

◆ Establish a fun and healthy competition with your other periods or classes.

◆ Increase students' Self-Awareness and help them find their voice by having lanyards available on your desk for daily student use. Lanyards can read: "I'm in Silent Practice," "Loving the silence," or "My solution today is silence" and you can invite students to wear them throughout the day, when they are walking in the hallway, or other times throughout the day when they may have a difficult time self-regulating. This is an especially useful tool if students are having a Thumbs-Down day. It is a safe, productive method to help students give themselves permission to unplug verbally without withdrawing from the school community. The lanyard informs people that the student is choosing silence today and that their lack of communication isn't being disrespectful. (The last thing you want is a toxic standoff between that student and an adult in the building that has not been made aware of the student's option to choose silence for the day.) This strategy also works well if your students eat breakfast or lunch in your classroom.

Restorative Practices: This activity is a great way to give students who are having a difficult time managing conflict the space to step back and reflect on their role within your classroom community. Take the time to frame the activity with the Agreements and the intention behind the practice ("We are engaging in Silent Practice today to …") to guarantee safety so that each student feels seen and respected. Conclude the activity with a Goal Setting Postcard (p. 139) to help solidify a positive path for moving forward.

Proud of Myself Postcard

✓ SOCIAL: Focus

Supplies: Index card to add the activity to the POP Chart
4×6 index cards
Postage stamps (optional)
Pens and pencils

Time: 7 minutes

Provide students with the "Why" of the activity: *We are creating* **Proud of Myself Postcards** *today to reinforce* **community-building, self-inquiry, self-esteem, and managing vulnerability.** *This activity empowers us to find our voices and witness our kind, compassionate selves as well as be kind and compassionate toward others.*

To begin, distribute 4×6 index cards to your students. Then, read the directions below aloud while your students follow along.

First: *Take a deep breath, and think of a reason you are proud of yourself, such as for being an attentive listener, a compassionate friend, or a good teammate.*

Then: *On the front of the index card (the side with lines), write a few sentences, or draw a picture, to illustrate why you are proud of yourself.*

Next: *Complete the back of the postcard (the side without lines) writing the reason you are proud of yourself today. Don't forget to sign and date your postcard!*

Last: *Address your postcard to someone with whom you would like to share your positive thoughts, such as a former teacher, a coach, a dean, a parent or caregiver, or a community member.*

> ★ **Restorative Practices:** This activity is a great way to build community in challenging times. I love using this strategy as a jumping off point for a Talking Stick circle. Have the students share their postcards, citing all they have to be proud of, or positive about, in the face of adversity. Take the time to frame the activity with the Agreements and the intention behind the practice ("We're sharing our Proud of Myself Postcards today to celebrate our strengths in this time of adversity …") to guarantee safety so that each student feels heard and respected. Conclude the activity with Memory Minute (p. 110) to give them a moment of mindful reflection before transitioning to the next activity.

Cause and Effect Drawing

✓ **SOCIAL: Focus**

Supplies: Index card to add the activity to the POP Chart
4×6 index cards or scratch paper
Pen or pencils

Time: 5 minutes

Provide students with the "Why" of the activity: *We are practicing* **Cause and Effect Drawing** *to explore the connections between our* **Social Awareness and our compassion for self and others**. *Cause and Effect Drawing builds awareness of ourselves in relation to others and the common feelings we all experience.*

First: Begin the activity by discussing the concepts of Compassion, Empathy, and other feelings or emotions from the POP Chart such as Happy, Angry, or Vulnerable. Write keywords on the board.

Then: Students record (write or draw) how **x** emotion or feeling that they have experienced is similar to **y** emotion that one of their peers has experienced: "I understand why Cameron was so frustrated (**x**) that his dad missed his birthday. I haven't seen my dad in four years and it really makes me angry (**y**)." Or, if you would like to tie the activity to academic content, such as *Death of a Salesman*: "I understand why Biff Loman yells, 'We haven't told the truth for ten minutes in this house!' out of frustration (**x**). Sometimes I feel like there are a lot of lies or unspoken realities in my house. This makes me feel helpless, sad, and vulnerable (**y**), just like Biff."

Next: The students find a Thought Partner (see p. 65) to share their drawings.

Last: Ask the students to review what they have written and drawn. Then, ask them to sit up tall and close their eyes. For 1 minute, ask the students to *"Visualize yourselves Being the Solution in your Cause and Effect Drawing."* If time permits, engage the class in a Talking Stick Discussion (p. 63) to close the activity. Ask a few students to share quick thoughts about their experience in this activity.

★ **Restorative Practices:** This activity is a great way to build community and manage conflict. I love using this strategy as a jumping off point for a Talking Stick circle. Take the time to frame the activity with the Agreements and the intention behind the practice ("Once complete, we will be sharing our Cause and Effect Drawings in a Talking Stick circle so that…") to guarantee safety so that each student feels heard and respected. Conclude the activity with a mindfulness practice, like Memory Minute, to help students find a focused, centered place before transitioning to the next lesson.

Goal Setting Postcard

✓ **SOCIAL: Focus**

Supplies: Index card to add the activity to the POP Chart
3 × 5 index cards, lined on one side
Pen or pencil

Time: 7 minutes

Provide students with the "Why" of the activity: *Today, we are creating **Goal Setting Postcards** to help us be **personally responsible and accountable**. This activity is great for reminding us that we are the creative principle in our own lives. We can Be the Solution when we feel frustrated or are facing a challenging task.*

First: Write the following template on the board for the students to copy.

"In the next two weeks I will _____ [action

verb] at _____ [time/day] because _____ [reason for

action].

    My classmate _____ [name of peer] will help me reach my

goal, if I need support.

    One bad habit or problem I will need to watch out for is _____

[potential problem]. I can Be the Solution by _____ [action

verb].

    Signed: _____   Date: _____

    Witnessed: _____   Date: _____

Then: On the front of the index card (the side with lines), ask the students to copy the template and find a Thought Partner to complete their goal with them.

Next: On the back of the index card (the side without lines), ask the students to write four to six sentences about why they chose that as their goal. How will that goal empower them to Be the Solution in their own lives?

Last: Once their Goal Setting Postcards are complete, ask the students to review what they have written. Then, ask them to sit up tall and close their eyes or pick a spot to focus their gaze. For 1 minute, ask the students to visualize what it would look, feel, and sound like to meet their goal. Ask students to *"Visualize yourselves Being the Solution and reaching your goal."* Once the minute concludes, ask for a few students to give you a one-word check-in, sharing one word about their goal or the activity.

★ **Teacher Tip:** This is a great pre-teaching activity for the Community-Based Service Learning Project (see p. 141) or for students who need help setting behavioral goals. You and the student can complete the Goal Setting Postcard together. You can revisit the postcard with the student weekly to offer support and/or until the goal has been realized.

Restorative Practices: This activity is a great way to conclude a Talking Stick circle or Shoulder Share session. Use this tool to set goals for your classroom community or to help your students, as a collective, overcome obstacles that are negatively impacting their learning environment.

Expansion Project:
Community-Based Service Learning Project

✓ SOCIAL: Focus

Supplies: To be determined based upon project chosen

Estimated project time: 3–4 weeks

Provide students with the "Why" of the activity: *We are planning and participating in a* **Service Learning Project** *to connect with our community by sharing thoughts and resources. In our SEL program this year we have worked hard to cultivate our sense of* **Self-Efficacy and Social Harmony by developing our leadership, collaboration, teamwork, and peer-to-peer communication skills**. *This year, we have worked on Being the Solution for ourselves and our school. Now, to demonstrate our Social-Emotional Learning skills, we will create a Service Learning Project to Be the Solution for our community.*

Service Learning Project: Having students work collaboratively to create a Service Learning Project is the perfect way to reinforce a sense of community. Service Learning Projects are most successful when they bring different groups together, such as one classroom partnering with an older/younger grade to create a school "Green Space" or to put on a play at the local senior center.

This project can become a growth narrative for the class and a reflection tool that validates their ability to foster effective interpersonal communication, to seize opportunities for self-reflection, and to accept the needs and limits of self and others.

Prior to the start of the project, it is important to message the concept of responsible giving and/or "giving back" to the community. Instead of framing the Service Learning Project as a one-sided proposition of "us" helping "them," discuss the ways in which "giving back" creates an opportunity for the class to contemplate their roles within the community, to share their voices with and listen to stakeholders, to collaborate with new partners, and to engage in a relationship of reciprocal learning. It is also crucial that the students set goals around the project, measure its impact, and examine prospects for sustainability, thus moving away from monetary gifts and moving toward "Being the Solution" and "giving back" via human connection.

★ **Teacher Tip:** Some states, such as Illinois, have Service Learning Standards that connect nicely to their Social-Emotional Learning standards (in this case, most notably, "Goal 3 – Demonstrate decision-making skills and responsible behaviors in personal, school, and community contexts"). Connecting these standards can be a great way to create metrics to measure the overall impact of the project. This project is also an excellent opportunity to build bridges between regular education students and students with exceptionalities!

9

Crafting SEL Stories

The SEL Story is an instrumental element of each teacher's approach to SEL. It is not the reading of the story or the theme of the story itself, it is the peer-to-peer communication tools employed during the activity that are the richest and most impactful aspect.

There are **two options** for how you may implement SEL Stories in your classroom.

Be the Solution Teams

The students work in teams to decide a solution to a culturally relevant SEL problem or issue taken from the POP Box.

Class Dialogue

The teacher uses one of the templates from pp. 147 or 148 to create a culturally relevant SEL Story based upon problems or issues taken from the POP Box. Or, the teacher reads one of the scripted SEL Stories provided and facilitates a reflective dialogue with the students.

Before choosing which option will work best, reflect on happenings in the school community that may or may not need to be addressed. Look at the interpersonal needs of your students and what would best serve them at present. Look at the time available for your lesson: the pacing of the activity is important and should not be rushed, as it will lose its reflective potency.

As the teacher delivering the lesson, reflect on your own SEL competency around the topic. What lessons have you learned that you can share with your students? What are your current challenges and areas of growth around the topic?

Implementation steps for both SEL options are outlined below. Some of the SEL terminology embedded in the Sample Stories (p. 148) is shown in **bold** to make it easy to emphasize during instruction. Transparency is key for SEL to take root in students' lives. The terminology should be used as part of a common classroom language during SEL instruction and across disciplines, and should be reinforced throughout the day.

Delivery of SEL Stories

Step 1: Look at the POP Chart. Where did the majority of students place their magnets? Which emotion or feeling is most represented in your class today and what do your students need to be present?

Step 2: Choose the SEL Story format:

◆ Option A: Be the Solution Teams
◆ Option B: Class Dialogue

Step 3: Close the activity with a Memory Minute to give your students an opportunity to reflect on what was shared, before moving onto their next class.

Message the "Why" to Your Students

The text in italic type below is a scripted lesson for introducing the SEL Stories to your students. As with the other scripted lessons in this book, it is **not** recommended that you read the script aloud word-for-word, as that would not help develop your competency as a practitioner. Instead, the script is meant to provide a solid idea of how the content is framed, paced, and managed. Read the script a few times, take notes, and then make it your own.

[Teacher writes Social-Emotional Learning on the board.] *As part of our Social-Emotional Learning program in Room [x] we will share* *real-life stories about Social-Emotional Learning every Monday. We will explore a new story or theme every week and discuss how it relates to Social-Emotional Learning and our own experiences as students at [x] High School. When big things are happening at school or in our community, we will get into Be the Solutions teams and discuss our SEL Story. Other days, when someone has added a question to the POP Box that we need to address as a class, we will have a conversation about the SEL Story and try to understand the story from different points of view. It is very important that the concepts and themes we discuss are relevant to you. Remember, you can always add a theme, idea, or concern to our POP Box if you would like me to include it as an SEL topic next week. Also, remember that we have the POP Chart to help us **PAUSE** and notice what we are feeling in the body and the mind.* [Teacher motions to POP Chart.] *So that we can **OWN** what we are feeling and **PRACTICE** a solution that meets our needs. We are in control of our choices. We can Be the Solution!*

Does anyone have any questions about our SEL Stories or our SEL time each week?

[Teacher observes classroom and answers questions.]

Option A: Be the Solution Teams

*Today, we will be using our creative thinking skills to come up with solutions for a Social-Emotional Learning scenario that was put in the POP Box. By working as a team to come up with a solution, we are using our **problem-solving and collaboration skills**. When we are discussing solutions, let's remember the tools we have learned using the POP Chart. Before we get started, we will be practicing a quick centering activity, so we have productively used our extra energy and can focus and work as a team.*

First: Select a student to lead your class through 10 focused breaths.

Practicing a quick centering activity is a great way to help the class release excess energy that can often make working in a group challenging for your more frenetic students.

Then: Write an SEL scenario from the POP Box on the board with two or three possible solutions. Place students in groups of four or five, and designate a Recorder and First Speaker (e.g., choosing a student with the shortest/longest hair, shortest first/last name, or birthday closest/furthest from today). When you say "Begin," the First Speaker will have 1 minute to share their opinion on which scenario is the best solution to the problem, while the Recorder takes notes.

Next: At the end of the minute, say "Switch" and, moving counterclockwise, the next student in the group will share their thoughts. This continues for five rounds, until each student has had a chance to speak. While the group is sharing, the Recorder is taking notes.

Last: Once the rounds have concluded, give the groups 3 minutes to synthesize their information and prepare to present it to the class. The Recorder will read her notes aloud. Starting with the First Speaker, the group will take turns adding any additional thoughts or solutions. When time is up, each group will have 1 minute to share their thoughts with the class. The Recorder may speak, or choose someone in the group to speak in her place.

In order for this exercise to have impact, students must feel the activity was relevant to their lives and has an effect on their immediate circumstances. The role of the teacher is key to build consensus and keep transitions tight. Besides the major benefits of tailor-making relevant SEL content for your classroom, the speaking and listening inherent in this activity are great for building interpersonal relationships among students.

This is an excellent activity for helping students take ownership of their behavior and find solutions in real time. For instance, if your students misbehave at an assembly, when you return to your classroom, put the students in their Be the Solution Teams and have them build consensus around a consequence and/or solution. This not only helps students develop a sense of personal responsibility, but it also helps them see the impact of their actions, both positive and negative, on the classroom community.

★ **Teacher Tip:** The script for creating the Agreements mentioned below is on p. 60, and would be a great way to create a safe space for this activity.

Decide how you would like to conclude the discussion. Did the class build consensus around a solution that you would like to add to your classroom Agreements? Would you like to revisit the process of adding a thought, concern, or idea to the POP Box as a way to inform the procedures and protocols of the classroom (and school) community? How can you engineer this activity to be both productive and reflective for you and the students? If there is space, perhaps keep an ongoing list of SEL competencies your class is practicing. Instead of the static and ineffective SEL "theme of the week," make this a living, breathing list that you are adding to, speaking to, and referencing throughout instruction.

Option B: Class Dialogue

Use the POP Box and the template below to write SEL Stories for your students. The more culturally relevant the stories are to the students' lives, the larger the impact. Sample reflection questions are also provided to conclude each lesson. In case you are having a difficult time getting started, I have included six sample SEL Stories later in the chapter.

Template 1

_____ (culturally relevant character name) is in the _____ class at

_____ school. _____ (name) found herself in a difficult situation

today. She _____ (name difficult situation). Because she

was upset, _____ (name) _____ (negative action), which is not a

positive step toward a solution. How can _____ (name) use one of the tech-

niques in the POP Chart to make a more positive choice? What solution would be a

more positive choice for _____ (name) and also help her be reflective?

Template 2

Today, _____ (culturally relevant character name) used poor decision-

making skills and got into trouble for _____. He/she knows that

it is his/her personal responsibility to resolve the situation. Unfortunately, he/she

_____ (negative action), which only made the problem worse.

Now _____ (name) does not know how to improve the situ-

ation. What is a positive way for _____ (name) to take responsibility for his/her

actions and find a solution? What Social-Emotional Learning tools or techniques

from our POP Chart could help him/her in this situation?

Template 3

Room _____ misbehaved today in _____. Their teacher is disappointed, because she knows that if they used better peer-to-peer communication and active listening skills, Room _____ could have made more positive choices about their behavior. To resolve the situation, Room _____ needs to reflect on their decision-making skills and use teamwork to find a positive next step. What are two positive steps that Room _____ could take to resolve the situation? How can they use Social-Emotional Learning or mindfulness strategies to find the most positive path?

Sample SEL Stories

SEL words are shown in **bold**. Check your POP Box weekly for students' questions and concerns. That is perfect fodder for timely and culturally relevant material to be converted to SEL Stories to share with class each Friday or during a Talking Stick discussion. *Scripted questions are in italic type below* to facilitate meaningful discussion around the themes of the SEL Stories with your students.

1. Zak was in the school musical on Thursday. He sang a solo and rode a skateboard across stage – doing a quick little kickflip. He was **nervous** about performing in front of his classmates and his brother, Jason, kept **teasing** him. When he returned to school on Friday, a few of his classmates told him he had done a good job. Zak **felt anxious** from **the attention** of his classmates and was really **proud** of himself. He was so glad that he didn't let Jason's teasing keep him from **pursuing his passion**.

May I have a volunteer to tell me what happens in the story? [Teacher asks one student to explain the story.]

*Now, may I have two volunteers to explain which techniques Zak could have practiced to help him deal with being **stressed and nervous**?* [Teacher asks two students to connect the SEL Story to the activities in the POP Chart. Once the students conclude, the teacher closes the activity by rephrasing their explanations in one or two sentences.]

2. Jamal was scheduled to play in the varsity basketball game after school and was so **excited** he was **having a hard time** focusing in class. He wanted to talk to his friends about the game! Jamal's teacher, Ms. Ruiz, was **frustrated** that she had to speak to him twice about his **disruptive behavior** and yelled at him to be quiet. Instead of turning to his friend and saying, "Ms. Ruiz is a jerk, she is ALWAYS yelling at me for NO reason," he paused for a moment, took three deep **breaths,** and tried to **observe the situation from an outside perspective**. Jamal apologized to Ms. Ruiz and explained the situation. Ms. Ruiz was impressed with Jamal's ability to **positively work through his feelings**. She thought Jamal's **calm down** strategy would work well for other students and so she asked Jamal to lead the class in a few quick, relaxing **breaths** before they moved on to the next part of their lesson.

May I have a volunteer to tell me what happens in the story? [Teacher asks one student to explain the story.]

*Now, may I have two volunteers to explain which techniques Jamal success-fully used to own his feelings, **make positive choices about his behavior, and be responsible for his actions**?* [Teacher asks two students to connect the SEL Story to the activities in the POP Chart. Once the students conclude, the teacher closes the activity by rephrasing students' explanations in one or two sentences.]

3. Katie was one of the best players on her basketball team. But, anytime her team started to fall behind in a game, she had the habit of taking a shot every time she got the ball. This **frustrated** her teammates, because the rest of them passed the ball **fairly** around the group. One girl on Katie's team, Reba, wanted to slap the ball out of Katie's hands. Instead, Reba talked to Katie about her **feelings of anger and frustration**. Although the conversation was difficult, both girls **managed their emotions** and neither one started a fight. After taking the time to **communicate**, Katie, Reba, and the other girls all started to **play together** much better and the team began to win more games.

May I have a volunteer to tell me what happens in the story? [Teacher asks one student to explain the story.]

*Now, may I have two volunteers to explain which techniques Reba could have practiced to help her **deal with her feelings of anger and frustration** before she* *talked to Katie?* [Teacher asks two students to connect the SEL Story to the activities in the POP Chart. Once the students conclude, the teacher closes the activity by rephrasing their explanations in one or two sentences.]

4. Jose is on his school's track team and always **tries his best** during practices and races. At the recent state championship, he tripped about 30 feet from the finish line, badly bruised his knee, and could not finish the race. After the championship, Jose's friend, Patrick, jokingly said, "Well, at least you remembered to wear sunblock." Jose yelled, "Leave me alone. I am a **failure**. I should have done better. I am a loser." Seeing the **sad** look on Patrick's face, Jose now **felt even worse** for snapping at his friend and **hurting his feelings**. But, he was **too upset to think clearly** and repair the situation.

May I have a volunteer to tell me what happens in the story? [Teacher asks one student to explain the story.]

Now, may I have two volunteers to explain which techniques Jose could have practiced to help him manage his feelings of anger and disappointment so that he didn't take them out on his friend Patrick? [Teacher asks two students to connect the SEL Story to the activities in the POP Chart. Once the students conclude, the teacher closes the activity by rephrasing their explanations in one or two sentences.]

5. Cathy's parents didn't go to college and they didn't understand why she wanted to go. Her parents would often say rude things to Cathy like, "Do you think you are better than us because you are going to go to college!?" Or, "What is wrong with the way you were raised? You think you are SO smart, don't you!?" Her parents' rude comments made Cathy **feel misunderstood.** She fought a lot with her parents and, because she felt a weird combination of shame and guilt, she often lacked motivation and stopped doing her homework. She wanted to go to college one day, but she needed to have a clear head and heart to start **focusing** on schoolwork. Cathy was **sad and frustrated**. She knew she needed to work really hard to get good grades, but she **felt alone and without any emotional support**.

May I have a volunteer to tell me what happens in the story? [Teacher asks one student to explain the story.]

Now, may I have two volunteers to explain which techniques Cathy can practice to help her **manage her feelings of frustration** *so she can be* **personally responsible for her actions?** [Teacher asks two students to connect the SEL Story to the activities in the POP Chart. Once the students conclude, the teacher closes the activity by rephrasing their explanations in one or two sentences.]

6. Gilda knew that when she did poorly on a test, it was important to be **compassionate with herself**. The most important thing was to **reflect on her mistakes** and keep **trying her best**. Instead of thinking unkind thoughts about herself, she would try to **think positive things** such as, "I am **proud** of myself for trying my best" or "I **worked really hard** even though I didn't get the grade I wanted." Gilda knows it is important to be compassionate with herself and others, even when times are hard and you want to find someone or something **to blame**.

May I have a volunteer to tell me what happens in the story? [Teacher asks one student to explain the story.]

Now, may I have two volunteers to explain which techniques Gilda can practice to help her **be more kind and compassionate with herself?** [Teacher asks two students to connect the SEL Story to the activities in the POP Chart. Once the students conclude, the teacher closes the activity by rephrasing their explanations in one or two sentences.]

10

The Power of Professional Development

Building Teacher Competency

Before we begin to assemble that first SEL bulletin board, we must take a look at our SEL competency, as teachers. Often when I am touring a new school, a principal will say this teacher has "got it" or that teacher "doesn't." In education-speak, we often are complicit at letting it go at just that. The problem is that without codifying the practices that create a positive, safe, and emotionally respectful classroom, we leave ourselves unable to teach those who haven't quite "got it" yet.

To mindfully implement SEL in our schools, it is time to move away from sweeping and lofty expectations like "teaching respect" toward building teachers' SEL competency by developing common, straightforward SEL language and practices for our classrooms. Our SEL instruction must dig deeper than simply looking at the number of students reached or the number of minutes taught. Instead, we must look at the competency of those who are the delivery vehicle for the SEL program itself. What is the climate and culture of the classroom in which the SEL program is housed? Is that classroom an emotionally and physically safe environment for SEL to take place, and can all learners, even our most vulnerable, thrive?

Teacher competency is a vital part of the successful implementation of a school-wide SEL program. If classroom teachers are expected to implement SEL programs and state SEL standards with efficacy, proficiency cannot be assumed. Given that most teacher education programs lack sufficient pre-service training in SEL, teachers must receive high-quality SEL PD, consistent support, and a safe space to reflect and take risks.

When I was a high school teacher, I knew whether or not I could effectively teach trigonometry. (I couldn't, I was certified in English and History.) The process is not as simple for teaching and assessing SEL. Many of our nation's teachers were certified before SEL was included in the state standards and so it was not included in their teacher education programs. When addressing educators' SEL competency at a new school site, I often hear the question, "Are you saying that some teachers don't know how to effectively resolve a conflict? Or that they don't have self-awareness?" And, as we think about how gossipy our faculty lounge can be at lunchtime, sometimes that answer is obvious.

Teachers cannot effectively teach SEL – or any content – without modeling. And they cannot effectively model what they are not competent in. Yet, at least half of the SEL instruction I see when I visit schools across the country is teachers pulling a card from a box or clicking and "teaching their SEL minutes for the day." The teacher's self-reflective piece is completely absent and the impact of the program is diminished. Or, at worst we dismiss SEL instruction as "one more thing we don't have time for," or "the flavor of the month." Desperate to include SEL in some fashion, schools often settle for the half-taught lesson in lieu of the content being abandoned all together. (Or put the burden of teaching SEL on the school social worker – who is already spread too thin.)

As I discuss in Chapter 1, the best practice here is to adopt a district-wide SEL and mindfulness **approach**, instead of simply buying a program and believing that is where the initiative stops. Address the question of teacher competency prior to getting started and insist upon PD as the cornerstone of an impactful and sustainable SEL initiative. Implementing an intentional and reflective PD program is key. A "one-shot" train-the-trainer PD session is not enough, as there is only time to cover particular SEL strategies, not to evaluate the practitioner's overall mastery of the concepts. One can learn "Chopsticks" on the piano, but that does not mean one can model proper classical piano technique or knows how to effectively teach "Chopsticks" to someone else.

Intentional PD gives us the space to view ourselves through the SEL lens. Are we self-aware? Are we able to self-regulate? What triggers us and keeps us from being present and compassionate educators?

Teachers cannot model or teach Self-Awareness or Self-Regulation in a school culture that doesn't honor these concepts as values. As John Hattie astutely observes in his book, *Visible Learning: A Synthesis of over 800 Meta-Analyses Relating to Achievement* (2009):

> School leaders and teachers need to create school, staffroom, and classroom environments where error is welcomed as a learning opportunity, where discarding incorrect knowledge and under-standings is welcomed, and where participants can feel safe to learn, re-learn, and explore knowledge and understanding.

To build an impactful SEL program, the "incorrect knowledge" that teachers, just by virtue of being teachers, are SEL competent must be discarded. How can we be competent in something that we have never been taught? This is the perfect storm that subverts teacher SEL competency: a high-stakes testing culture that doesn't make space for vulnerability, an emotion-averse system that glorifies "busy," and a lack of high-quality, experiential SEL training. Our teachers often feel they are "running on fumes" and do not have time for "one more thing," even if implementing that one more thing – Social-Emotional Learning – would help them and their students be more engaged and thus achieve more (the very thing that is stressing teachers out in the first place). As an educational community, we need to slow down, give teachers the space and time to reflect, be present, and take care of their mental, emotional, and physical needs. Because if teachers have not experienced the value of self-care, they won't find time for it in their classrooms. If schools provide teachers with a safe space to reflect on their own SEL competency, they will be empowered to master the content they are expected to deliver.

Building an Impactful Professional Development Experience

Step 1: Recruit Your Principal

One of the jobs of an administrator is to create an emotionally and physic-ally safe space for his team to have room to be creative, reflective, and to take risks. Teachers must be given permission to move away from the nar-rative of "too busy" or "too disenchanted" to care. We should frame this shift the same way we give the challenging student permission to reinvent his self-perpetuating label of "Class Clown," so that he can abandon the shackles of the narrative and grow in a more positive direction.

It is vital that the administration introduces the PD program and mes-sages expectations around SEL at the school. With all the other things on teachers' plates at the start of the school year, why should they be expected to devote time to a 3-hour SEL PD session? Why has the district allocated valuable resources for this work? What is our baseline? What are the expectations? What is the timeline? How is this connected to student achievement? And, of course, how will SEL be reflected in teacher evaluations?

If the principal is not ready to answer these questions, then the implementation will lack commitment. Implementing SEL with integrity takes strong leadership, consistently reinforced boundaries, difficult conversations, and clear vision.

This is a great opportunity to work alongside your principal or superintendent to create the school's SEL plan. Before moving forward with implementation, take time to sit with your administrator to discuss the questions below, so that you can deliver a clear and consistent message to the school stakeholders at the first PD session.

Question 1: The game plan
What is your vision for our school's SEL program?

Question 2: The timeline
What is our timeline and what steps do we need to take to get there?

Question 3: The measurement
How do we track our progress to make sure we stay on course?

Question 4: The team
Who are the school SEL stakeholders that can lead the charge and help us create something sustainable?

Question 5: The wish list
What resources and support do we need to accomplish our vision?

Question 6: Common language
How do we frame SEL to our school community – teachers, bus drivers, parents, administrators, lunch monitors, deans, social workers, etc. – so it reinforces the SEL vision for our school?

Question 7: Call to Action
In the Zone? Be the Solution? Ready to Learn? How can all school stakeholders consistently message expectations to our students?

Question 8: Service Learning Project
Brainstorm an end-of-year Service Learning Project that brings our school into connection with our community and reinforces SEL concepts, like teamwork and compassion.

If the principal cannot be the leadership presence at each SEL PD session, it is important that he chooses a strong facilitator to lead the charge and help participants Be In the Zone in his absence.

Step 2: Choose a Strong PD Facilitator

The role of the facilitator is of utmost importance for a successful PD session, for it is her job to create an emotionally and physically safe space for learning to take place. Often, when I am leading a PD session, I will have an observer say to me, "Well, um, do we really need the Agreements [see p. 160]? I mean, these are adults, and they might be offended." My answer is, predictably, YES.

Typically, it is those participants that are offended by the Agreements that need them the most. They are the participants that invade boundaries and make others feel uncomfortable or unsafe by grading papers when the facilitator is speaking, making rude comments under their breath, showing up late, chomping on a snack, or checking their phones – anything that keeps them from being present. All these actions send the message that they don't need the content and don't think it is worth their time to be there. The role of the facilitator takes courage. It takes guts. It takes grit and the willingness to have difficult conversations. No more "Well, that's just Coach Butler *being* Coach Butler." Rude participants are exhibiting behavior they would never tolerate from their students. It is the job of the facilitator to create boundaries and set limits so that the PD is safe for all.

Facilitators must be comfortable modeling the strategies during the PD session that they want their teachers to model in their classrooms, if they expect sustainable, school-wide implementation. Be the Solution, or your Call to Action, must apply to all stakeholders – no exceptions. A successful PD experience, facilitated in a safe environment by a strong, consistent voice, will pull disenfranchised teachers back into connection with one another and with their profession.

Step 3: Create an Implementation Timeline for PD in SEL

Design a timeline for PD in SEL that spans from August to June. Allow time for reflection to help build a sustainable program that reaches every stakeholder in every corner of the school building.

Before the start of the school year, make sure the following actions have been taken, using the information gathered from the principal (see Step 1 above), to build a solid foundation for PD programming.

1. Rally stakeholders and establish an SEL PD committee.
2. Review and revisit your state's SEL standards, the Call to Action (i.e., "Be the Solution"), and the school's SEL vision.
3. Conduct a needs assessment or pre-survey. Design a Common Language Document reflecting the marriage between school priorities, state SEL standards, and the school's SEL vision. Build consensus around teacher expectations (see Table 10.1) and adopt a rubric (p. 20).
4. Create a PD Calendar (see sample below). Send out a newsletter to school stakeholders introducing the SEL program and inviting all to attend the PD workshops. Keep an updated calendar and sign-in sheets, and incentivize participation.
5. Give teachers the time and resources to create SEL classrooms, including POP Charts and Call to Action messaging.

Sample PD and Committee Meeting Calendar

August: SEL Committee Meeting – Establishing Baseline, Practices, and Expectations
September: PD Session 1
October: SEL Committee Meeting – Reviewing and Refining Practices and Expectations
November: PD Session 2
January: SEL Committee Meeting – Assessment of Skills Learned: Where are we and what do we need to improve?
February: PD Session 3
April: SEL Committee Meeting – Ongoing Implementation Assessment: How have we grown? What type of Service Learning Project would celebrate our growth?
May: PD Session 4
June: SEL Committee Meeting – Ongoing Implementation Assessment: **Have we created a sustainable approach to SEL?**

Table 10.1 Competencies for School Stakeholders

SEL Competency	"Looks Like, Sounds Like, Feels Like"	Strategies to Build SEL Competency
Self-Awareness ◆ Self-esteem, positive self-talk, personal responsibility, and emotional awareness ◆ Body awareness and healthy lifestyle choices	◆ "I matter. I make a difference in students' lives. I set the tone for my classroom" ◆ "I OWN that my stress impacts my students. I am a powerful model of behavior" ◆ "It is my responsibility to model self-care and healthy lifestyle choices for my students" *Move from powerlessness to empowered*	◆ Brain Massage ◆ Seated Yoga Sequence ◆ Standing Yoga Sequence ◆ Write and Rip
Self-Regulation ◆ Managing and expressing emotions appropriately	◆ "I reflect on my role in our school and the attitude I bring to situations" ◆ Adaptability, coping skills, and problem-solving ◆ "I choose to find solutions and think creatively so that all needs are met" *Move from impulsivity to positivity*	◆ Five-Part Breath ◆ Still Point ◆ Mooka Meditation ◆ Memory Minute
Social Awareness ◆ Active listening skills, empathy, and community-building	◆ "I know that I am a valued member of the school community and am aware that my positive energy, participation and collaboration impact those around me" *Move from reactive and victimized to proactive and collaborative*	◆ Cooperation Circle ◆ Compliment Partners ◆ Shoulder Share ◆ Boom Board!
Balance between Self-Efficacy and Social Harmony ◆ Leadership, collaboration, teamwork ◆ Compassion with self and others	◆ "I appreciate the importance of teamwork and value my role in our school community. I chose to collaborate with others to Be the Solution, not the problem" ◆ "I can manage vulnerability. I have found my voice and am comfortable and confident expressing my needs." ◆ "I realize that being compassionate with myself, my students, and my colleagues is one of the most important things I do as an educator" *Effectively balancing the needs of the SELF with the needs of the group (SOCIAL) – without self-sacrifice*	◆ Goal Setting Postcard ◆ Compliment Partners ◆ Talking Stick ◆ Check-In and Pass the Squeeze Circle

Step 4: Create an Emotionally and Physically Safe PD Environment

Creating an emotionally and physically safe space is a critical element of a successful PD session. Often, PD takes place in the library or school cafeteria and very little is done to "set the stage" for sharing and reflection.

Included in the "Materials needed" in the Facilitator's Guides in the next chapter are supplies that model the Agreements and the other communication tools found in teachers' SEL classrooms. Using these tools during PD not only provides the teachers with a safe space to learn, it also experientially walks them through the same process as a learner that they are facilitating as a practitioner.

The Agreements below are adapted from those developed by my dear friend Mario Rossero, who is at the Kennedy Center in Washington, DC. I find them exceptionally useful for framing any adult learning experience, as they "create a safe space for dialogue and critical conversation and aim to create equity of voice and ideas for sharing and growth."

The classroom sample Agreements are on p. 60, but I have included an alternative version below specifically designed for PD. To practice cultural competency when introducing the Agreements, I like to invite the session participants to offer amendments before we move forward. As many cultures have different conversational norms, this is a great way to build consensus around creating a safe space for all voices to be heard. Once the session has begun, however, the Agreements must be upheld as they stand for the duration of the PD.

Enforcing the Agreements is not easy. As I have already suggested, it is usually the participant that needs the Agreements the most that is the most resistant to their use. This resistance can take the form of outbursts, diatribes, or insubordination. It is important that the facilitator is prepared to match strength with strength. If a person is violating the safe space created by the Agreements, it is the facilitator's responsibility to honor the needs of the group and either help shift that person's behavior, or escort them out of the session. The needs of the individual cannot trump the needs of the group, even if her voice is the loudest and most impassioned one in the room.

Professional Development Agreements

1. **Be fully present**
   No food, phones, laptops, or anything that may distract you from our session.

2. **Speak your truth as you know it now**
   Share only your story, not your friend's or something you heard.
3. **Accept non-closure and experience discomfort**
   Sometimes questions and concerns will be left without answers or resolution. Expect to leave your comfort zone.
4. **Remember the 24-hour rule**
   There are only 24 hours to resolve conflicts from the session. No grudges: let it go.
5. **Watch your air time: two and two**
   Two minutes maximum and two people speak before you share again. Original thoughts only: avoid piggybacking.
6. **Use our communication tools**
   Pants on Fire!, Talking Stick, Boom Board!, *Snaps*, and Table Taps.
7. ***Snaps* and Table Taps**
   Witness others' fabulousness and constructively find your voice when challenged or upset. Accept gentle reminders to help you be mindful of the Agreements.

★ **Teacher Tip:** *Snaps* = participants snap three times in the air when they agree with the speaker. Table Taps = participants tap their fingers on a table if they witness someone breaking the Agreements or making a generalization, such as "All middle school teachers in this district lack creativity."

As noted in number 6 above, I would also recommend Pants on Fire! (p. 67) and a Boom Board! (p. 65) for participants to share bright spots, challenges, or factors that are keeping them from being fully present.

Step 5: Implement Meaningful and Relevant PD Content

My organization, Mindful Practices, has been providing high-quality PD across the country since 2006 and I am proud to share with you our best practices. Agendas for three PD sessions, the Professional Development Facilitator's Guides, are outlined in Chapter 11.

If possible, implement the agendas in the time allotted and with the activities provided. The agendas are structured to build participant SEL competency from Self-Awareness to Self-Regulation to Social Awareness and on to find the balancing between Self-Efficacy and Social Harmony.

The sessions are experiential in nature and empower participants to read and respond proactively to their bodies' cues, to mirror the students' experience in the classroom. The union between the body and the mind is cultivated through four interconnected disciplines:

Vocalization: speaking, chanting, singing
Movement: gross/fine/locomotor, yoga, dance, fitness
Stillness: reflection, mindfulness, breath work, meditation
Community-building: play, collaboration, communication

As with all PD workshops, it is important that the pacing finds that delicate balance between modifying the content to meet the needs of the audience and maintaining the integrity of the delivery. Give the participants ample space to leave their comfort zones, be reflective, and take risks.

The Educator Pre-/Post-Survey (p. 174) should also be included to help teachers monitor their own progress. This tool can easily be adapted for student use as well, if an informal progress-monitoring tool is needed.

11

Executing the Professional Development Facilitator's Guides

Included in this chapter are three Facilitator's Guides utilizing the activities and materials in this book. The sessions are designed to be experiential in nature, not merely a "sit and get," and average between 2 hours and 30 minutes to 3 hours in length.

It is recommended that each teacher has a copy of *Everyday SEL* in hand during the PD session to make notes in real time after experientially participating in each activity. This process will help the teachers engage in "split vision" and mentally bridge the gap between learner and facilitator.

Professional Development Facilitator's Guide: Session 1

Beginning of the School Year

[School name]   [Date]

[Facilitator name and contact information]

Topic: Building Teacher Social-Emotional Learning Competency

> Relaxed teachers teach better. Relaxed students learn better.
> Tantillo and Crowley (2012)

Outcomes: By attending this session, practitioners will:

1. Build their knowledge of Social-Emotional Learning (SEL).
2. Develop their SEL competency by experientially practicing strategies.
3. Build consensus around what SEL *looks like, sounds like, and feels like* at [school name].
4. Develop the ability to model and encourage Self-Awareness and Self-Regulation in their classrooms, homes, and/or work with students.
5. Set goals for their implementation of SEL with consistency and fidelity.

Estimated time: 2.5–3 hours

Audience: [x] teachers, [x] administrators, [x] support staff, [x] parents/ community members, [x] school stakeholders and faculty

Materials needed: Chart paper, markers, copies of *Everyday SEL*, index cards, small sticky notes, photocopies of rubric (p. 20), Educator Pre-/Post-Survey (p. 174), and copy of your state's SEL standards, if applicable.

Room set-up: Boom Board! (p. 65), Pants on Fire! (p. 67), POP Chart (p. 73), POP Box (p. 61)

After each activity, the facilitator cues the participants to turn to the corresponding page in *Everyday SEL* to take notes in the margin. How can they amend the activity to work with their specific student population?

What modifications should they make to allow for space/time constraints, to align with their academic content, and to meet the needs of their students with exceptionalities?

SEL messaging by Principal [X]: Why are you all here? Why is SEL a priority at our school? What do I expect to see over what timeline, and how will these expectations be mirrored in your evaluations? What is our Call to Action? Would a Call to Action, such as "Being In the Zone," "Being the Solution," or "Being Ready to Learn," work for us and our students? What does "Being In the Zone" look like for you, as an educator? – 20 minutes

Facilitator begins
*Administer Educator Pre-Survey, if not already done.

1. Agreements for our PD session (p. 160) and using Agreements and Check for Understanding with your students (p. 62) – 20 minutes
2. The Mindful Practices approach (p. 9), Getting Started (p. 49), and your state's SEL standards, if applicable. What is our school's SEL goal? – 15 minutes
3. Brain Massage (p. 84) – 5 minutes
4. How to Use: Thumb Check (p. 74) – 3 minutes
5. How to Use: Boom Board! (p. 65) – 3 minutes
6. How to Use: Pants on Fire! (p. 67) – 3 minutes
7. Cooperation Circle (p. 116) into Pass the Clap Circle (p. 119) – 20 minutes
8. Talking Stick (p. 63): If you bumped into a former student at the grocery store, would you rather she remembered the details of the academic content you delivered ("My two favorite elements were Strontium and Scandium because …") or that she had the skills to hold down a job, maintain positive relationships, and be a productive, compassionate citizen of the world? How does implementing SEL in our classrooms help us create life-long learners and achievers? How can we model "Being the Solution" for our students daily? – 20 minutes
9. Crafting SEL Stories (p. 143) – 15 minutes
10. Seated Yoga Sequence (p. 85) – 10 minutes
11. Shoulder Share (p. 132): Review the SEL strategies you have learned so far today. Share how you can modify them to work with your students – 15 minutes
12. Ready to Learn Breath (p. 98) – 10 minutes

13. Debrief with Rubric (p. 20). Given what Principal [X] said at the beginning of our PD, what needs to be amended on the rubric to meet the specific needs of our school community? How can we message our SEL approach to other stakeholders in the building? – 15 minutes

14. Goal Setting Postcard (p. 139). [Participants copy template onto an index card which is collected by facilitator and passed out at the start of the next PD session.]

"In the next two weeks I will implement the following activities

with my students _____

[list of activities] at this time _____ [list times]

on these days _____ [list days]

because _____ [list rationale for using SEL

strategies]. My colleague _____ [write name of

Thought Partner] will help support me, if I need additional

resources and ideas." [Signed and dated by both participant

and Thought Partner.] – 20 minutes

15. Check-In and Pass the Squeeze Circle (p. 130) – 5 minutes

Professional Development Facilitator's Guide: Session 2

Middle of the School Year

[School name]   [Date]

[Facilitator name and contact information]

Topic: Building Teacher Social-Emotional Learning Competency

> Teaching is subject to compassion.
> Carla Tantillo Philibert, *Everyday SEL in Elementary School* (2016: 29)

Outcomes: By attending this session, participants will:

1. Build their knowledge of Social-Emotional Learning (SEL).
2. Develop their SEL competency by experientially practicing strategies.
3. Build consensus around what SEL *looks like, sounds like, and feels like* at [school name].
4. Model and encourage Self-Awareness, Self-Regulation, and Social Awareness in their classrooms, homes, and/or work with students.
5. Set goals for their implementation of SEL with consistency and fidelity.

Estimated time: 2.5–3 hours

Audience: [x] teachers, [x] administrators, [x] support staff, [x] parents/community members, [x] school stakeholders and faculty

Materials needed: Chart paper, markers, copies of *Everyday SEL*, index cards, small sticky notes, and photocopies of rubric

Room set-up: Boom Board! (p. 65), Pants on Fire! (p. 67), POP Chart (p. 73), POP Box (p. 61)

After each activity, the facilitator cues the participants to turn to the corresponding page in *Everyday SEL* to take notes in the margin. How can they amend the activity to work with their specific student population? What modifications should they make to allow for space/time constraints, to align with their academic content and to meet the needs of their students with exceptionalities?

Facilitator begins

1. Review Agreements, Check for Understanding, Thumb Check, Boom Board!, and Pants on Fire! – 15 minutes
2. Pass back Goal Setting Postcards. Debrief: Where am I with my goal? What are my successes? What are my challenges? Where do I need to ask for help? How can I support the school's SEL vision and help lay the foundation for a sustainable SEL approach for next year? – 15 minutes
3. Standing Yoga Sequence (p. 88) – 15 minutes
4. Pants on Fire! or Boom Board! – 5 minutes
5. Drawing Out Loud (p. 128) – 10 minutes
6. Write and Rip (p. 91) – 10 minutes
7. Talking Stick: Many states have adopted SEL standards without providing guidance on how teachers should be trained in SEL. Is that fair to teachers and students? Would standards for any other discipline, such as Music or Math, be adopted with the same assumption that all teachers are proficient in the delivery of that content? If you continue to reflect on your own SEL competency, where do you fall on the spectrum of Basic Needs ("fight or flight") to the Balance between Self-Efficacy and Social Harmony (see Figure 1.2)? – 20 minutes (principal stops in to facilitate, if possible).
8. Crafting SEL Stories (p. 143) – 15 minutes
9. Shoulder Share (p. 132): Review the SEL strategies you have learned so far today. Share how you can modify them to work with our students during state testing time – 15 minutes
10. Mooka Meditation (p. 102) – 10 minutes
11. Select a volunteer to teach one of the SEL strategies learned today to the group (delivered as if teaching students) – 15 minutes
12. Debrief with Rubric: Does anything need to be amended on the rubric? Are we on track to meet the needs of our school community by building a sustainable SEL approach for next year? – 10 minutes
13. Goal Setting Postcard [Collected by facilitator and passed out start of next PD session]

    "In the next two weeks I will implement the following activities

    with my students _____

    [list of activities] at this time _____ [list times]

    on these days _____ [list days]

because _____ [list rationale for using SEL

strategies]. My colleague _____ [write name of

Thought Partner] will help support me, if I need additional

resources and ideas." [Signed and dated by both participant

and Thought Partner.] – 15 minutes

14. Check-In and Pass the Squeeze Circle (p. 130) – 5 minutes

Professional Development Facilitator's Guide: Session 3

End of the School Year

[School name]   [Date]

[Facilitator name and contact information]

Topic: Building Teacher Social-Emotional Learning Competency

> School is concurrently a personal and interpersonal enterprise for students. To be successful, students must artfully navigate both arenas at once.
>
> Carla Tantillo Philibert

Outcomes: By attending this session, participants will:

1. Build their knowledge of Social-Emotional Learning (SEL).
2. Develop their SEL competency by experientially practicing strategies.
3. Build consensus around what SEL *looks like, sounds like, and feels like* at [school name].
4. Model and encourage Self-Awareness, Self-Regulation, Social Awareness, Self-Efficacy, and Social Harmony in their classrooms, homes, and/or work with students.
5. Set goals for their implementation of SEL with consistency and fidelity.

Estimated time: 2.5–3 hours

Audience: [x] teachers, [x] administrators, [x] support staff, [x] parents/ community members, [x] school stakeholders and faculty

Materials needed: Chart paper, markers, copies of *Everyday SEL*, index cards, small sticky notes, photocopies of rubric, and checklist

Room set-up: Boom Board! (p. 65), Pants on Fire! (p. 67), POP Chart (p. 73), Thumbs-Up/Thumbs-Down Box (p. 61)

After each activity, the facilitator cues the participants to turn to the corresponding page in *Everyday SEL* to take notes in the margin. How can they amend the activity to work with their specific student population? What modifications should they make to allow for space/time constraints, to align with their academic content and to meet the needs of their students with exceptionalities?

Facilitator begins
1. Review Agreements, Check for Understanding, Thumbs-Up/Thumbs-Down, Boom Board! and Pants on Fire! – 10 minutes
2. Review school's vision for SEL this school year. What is our capacity for the fall? What is sustainable? How can we involve more stakeholders in this work? – 15 minutes
3. Pass back Goal Setting Postcards. Debrief: Where am I with my goal? What do I need to amend? Where do I need support to build a sustainable practice for next school year? – 10 minutes
4. Index Card Scavenger Hunt (p. 124) – 10 minutes
5. Owning My Own Story Journal (p. 105) – 10 minutes
6. Talking Stick: To reinforce SEL's balance between Self-Efficacy and Social Harmony, the next step of the curriculum is for our students to work collaboratively on a Service Learning Project (p. 141). What could a Service Learning Project look like at our school? How can we utilize our Call to Action to "Be the Solution" for our school community? How can this help us build a sustainable SEL approach for next year? – 25 minutes
7. Five-Part Breath – 5 minutes
8. Crafting SEL Stories – 15 minutes
9. Shoulder Share: Review the SEL strategies you have learned so far today. Share how you can modify them to work with our students so they have self-comforting strategies to use over the summer – 10 minutes
10. Select a volunteer to teach one of the SEL strategies learned today to the group (delivered as if teaching students) – 10 minutes
11. Pants on Fire! or Boom Board! Break – 5 minutes
12. Compliment Partners (p. 126) – 10 minutes
13. Memory Minute (p. 110) – 5 minutes
14. Debrief with Rubric and checklist facilitated by Principal [X]: Now that it is the end of the school year, how have we met the needs of our school community? What are our successes? Have we fallen short? How have you expanded your SEL competency and grown as a practitioner? Have we built a sustainable SEL approach for next year? If not, what are our next steps? – 25 minutes

15. Final Goal Setting Postcard [Collected by principal and mailed to participants over the summer.]

> "Over the summer, I will reflect on how to revise and refine the following activities to use with my students _____ _____ [list of activities]. I will contact my colleague _____ [write name of Thought Partner] to help me brainstorm ways to build a sustainable SEL approach for my classroom. If I need additional resources, I will email Principal [x] by _____ [date] with ideas and potential solutions." [Signed and dated by participant, Thought Partner, and principal.] – 10 minutes

16. Check-In and Pass the Squeeze Circle (p. 130) – 5 minutes

* Administer Educator Post-Survey, if not already done.

Appendix

Educator Pre-/Post-Survey

Please Circle the Number That Best Describes Your Response

Name: Department: Date:

1. I understand how levels of energy (both my students' and mine) impact my classroom dynamic. I teach my students the life-long learning tools to relax, focus, and be present.

    1 Strongly disagree 2 Disagree 3 Agree 4 Strongly agree

2. I provide structure and effectively communicate procedures, protocols, and reinforce boundaries with my students daily.

    1 Strongly disagree 2 Disagree 3 Agree 4 Strongly agree

3. I articulate clear, reasonable expectations for my students. I manage my classroom with consistency and fairness.

    1 Strongly disagree 2 Disagree 3 Agree 4 Strongly agree

4. I encourage my students to make decisions about their own learning. We set tangible, explicit, and meaningful goals about learning and behavior. My students are empowered to Be the Solution.

    1 Strongly disagree 2 Disagree 3 Agree 4 Strongly agree

5. I honor the Social-Emotional Learning needs of my students. I include daily mindfulness, breathing, and movement/yoga activities that help my students and me focus, concentrate, and be Ready to Learn.

    1 Strongly disagree 2 Disagree 3 Agree 4 Strongly agree

6. I create a classroom climate of "respect and rapport" in which my students feel both emotionally and physically safe.

    1 Strongly disagree 2 Disagree 3 Agree 4 Strongly agree

7. I make choices about food and drink for myself and my students that model a healthy lifestyle.

    1 Strongly disagree 2 Disagree 3 Agree 4 Strongly agree

8. I reflect on my practices as an educator and work hard to develop my Social-Emotional Learning competency. I know what behaviors from colleagues and students trigger me. I model the behaviors I want my students to exhibit. I OWN that I am a role model.

    1 Strongly disagree 2 Disagree 3 Agree 4 Strongly agree

Additional Thoughts and Observations:

Questions from the Field

I began Mindful Practices in 2006 to empower teachers and students through SEL, yoga, and wellness to create a more effective educational environment. In that time, my team and I have worked with a diverse cohort of schools with varying needs. Below is a sampling of questions that we often receive during program implementation. If your question is not answered here, please feel free to contact me directly to brainstorm solutions. It is important to me that practitioners have the tools and resources to implement SEL with fidelity.

1. Problem: I am the only one implementing SEL and mindfulness at my school. When I approached my principal with this concept she said, "Go ahead and try it; if it works in your room, then we can talk about implementing it next semester." How can I develop my own SEL competency along with my students, if there is **no SEL PD** at my school?

Solution: First, share the PD material (Chapters 10 and 11) with your principal. Ask her if you can teach a lesson during your next institute or PD day. Then, offer a follow-up session before or after school for those teachers that are interested in learning more. This is great way to develop a small community of SEL innovators at your school site!

Additionally, along with practicing the SEL lessons you use with your students, you can also begin a reflective journal on these five areas of growth:

- ◆ Being explosive or emotionally reactive
- ◆ Advocating for personal or safe space
- ◆ Being compassionate with self and others
- ◆ Navigating difficult conversations
- ◆ Wrestling with perfectionism

Write in your reflective journal before school, after school, or during your preparatory period or your lunch. Any time you observe yourself or your students wrestling with or excelling on one of those five concepts, then cross-reference with the Educator Pre-/Post-Survey (p. 174) to reflect on your findings.

Don't forget to visit www.MindfulPracticesYoga.com to learn about our tech tool and self-care program for teachers!

2. Problem: I only use exercise or yoga videos with my students because my **classroom is so overcrowded**. I would love to use more authentic movement with students as part of their SEL time. How can I get them to stand without being on top of one another? And should I worry about parents' religious objections to yoga or mindfulness?

Solution: Each and every time you ask the students to stand, explicitly state and model your expectations: "In Room 304 we respect our peers' personal space. We respect our community by refraining from jokes or comments. We respect ourselves by listening to our bodies."

Instead of turning solely to online resources, I encourage educators to practice yoga with their students, such as the Seated or Standing Yoga Sequences (pp. 85 and 88) or the Movement Improv activity (p. 121). Besides being an outlet for teachers themselves to get a bit of stress-relieving exercise, it also easily transitions to a student-led activity, fostering student leadership and cooperation. Once the class becomes accustomed to the procedures and protocols surrounding the activity, it is easy to have students create movement sequences to share with the class.

As for parents' potential religious objections to yoga or mindfulness, it is always best to err on the side of caution and send a note home to parents, explaining that yoga is the union of body and mind and that mindfulness is a practice that helps us be "in the now," or the present moment. **Reassure them that no religion or prayer will be taught**, but explain that the students will be moving through poses and that parents should let the school know if they or their students are uncomfortable so that alternative accommodations can be made.

3. Problem: I am an administrator and I want to **start our day with a positive** breathing activity to build our school climate and culture. Any ideas?

Solution: Say the following as part of the announcements every morning.

> We try our best.
> We are self-aware.
> We are responsible for our own behavior.
> We matter.
> We are the Solution!

Then, roll into "We are – We are – the Solution (clap clap) – the Solution (clap clap)! We are – We are – the Solution (clap clap)! The Solution (clap clap)!"

(Sung to the tune of "We Will Rock You")

Depending on teachers' comfort levels, you can ask them to have students clap or pound on desks as a great way to let go of excess energy.

To begin class with centered energy, conclude the activity with 10 Ready to Learn Breaths (p. 98).

4. Problem: Many of my students **are victims of poverty, trauma, abuse, and/or are living in shelters or sleeping on couches** and have a difficult time with the concepts of **Personal Space, Boundaries, and Safe Touch.** Is there a way I can pre-teach the concepts before introducing movement into my classroom?

Solution: Yes! Thank you for addressing this concern! MANY schools do not cover these important concepts. DO NOT assume that the "Nurse at the local middle school taught this stuff a few years ago. These are high school kids, they *should* know this already." It is truly regrettable that many of our students leave school without any adult being brave enough to facilitate this difficult conversation. Read the scripts below. Highlight the parts that resonate for you and your students. After you have established the Agreements (Figure 4.2), use these pieces as a jumping-off point for a safe and open class discussion.

Plan ahead and invite the school social worker into your classroom for this discussion. Ask him to review the obligations of Mandated Reporter in your state. If time permits, close with a Talking Stick (p. 63) circle with students reinforcing the concepts of Personal Space, Boundaries, Safe Touch, etc. Explain to students that the rules of Personal Space, Boundaries, and Safe Touch apply at both school and home. Additionally, remind the students that they can put any questions, or concerns that they don't want to share with the entire class into the POP Box. [*Scripted material in italic type below.*]

Personal Space

Asking for Personal Space is creating a respectful boundary for yourself and those around you. Picture yourself in a situation when your physical or emotional space is not being respected. Maybe you are around someone who is getting too close and it doesn't feel right or it makes you feel weird in your body. Maybe someone is expressing their anger in a way that makes you feel unsafe. Or, maybe you are in a challenging situation where you feel like your voice is not being heard. Often, when we are in one of these situations, we don't say anything because we don't want to hurt the other person's feelings or cannot find our words. But, we must always remember that someone else's comfort is NEVER more important than our comfort. Even someone that is close to us – a cousin, a friend, an aunt or uncle, a coach, a parent – may need help remembering that EVERYONE deserves their own physical and emotional safe space. Take a breath and picture yourself asking for safe space. Find your voice. Use your words. Maybe you say, "Please stop. What you are doing doesn't make me feel safe." Or, "Please stop. I would like you take three steps back and honor my personal space." Take another breath and picture the other person hearing your request. He may be able to honor your request nicely, he may be confused and need an explanation, or he may get upset and be offended. However he responds, it doesn't mean that you were wrong to request personal space. It just means he was not ready to hear you. That is OK. You may need to firmly remind him again. Remember, everyone has a right to her own physical and emotional safe space.

Safe Touch and Boundaries

Safe Touch is a very personal thing. The rules of Safe Touch apply at school and at home. Just because someone is related to you, a close friend or an adult you "trust" does NOT mean that they can violate your sense of Safe Touch. Ever.

> *For me, Safe Touch is . . .*
> *Head to Shoulders.* [Teacher motions toward head, moves down to shoulders.]
> *Shoulders to Hands.* [Teacher motions toward shoulders, moves down to hands.]
> *Knees to Feet.* [Teacher motions toward knees, moves down to feet.]
> Repeat sequence.

Our sense of what our boundaries are and what we consider Safe Touch is often formed in childhood. People who have experienced trauma or abuse

– if we have or someone else in our lives – experience a loss of control over their own bodies. Victims of trauma or abuse often grow to adulthood having never learned boundaries or the basic rules of ownership of one's body. That is why it is critical that you learn to create boundaries for yourself, do not assume that adults or other students in your life "have boundaries" and "practice Safe Touch" simply because they are older than you or because they "seem OK."

If it is difficult for you to say "NO" to others when you would like to, say "Stop. Now!" and remove yourself from the situation. Immediately. Do not negotiate with him or her. You do not "owe them anything." Do not worry about taking care of their feelings or needs. You are not responsible for their emotions. No one's emotional, physical, or mental needs are more important than your own. Leave immediately and tell someone in a position of authority what happened.

5. Problem: I am a school administrator and I need more ideas on **including Be the Solution**, our Call to Action, across disciplines. I am having a hard time getting buy-in from our auxiliary staff.

Solution: Invite your **school community** to get involved in the school's daily routines, such as morning announcements. "Dorothy Adam High School, let's start our day the Be the Solution Way!"

School stakeholders are the faces that shape your students' educational experience. This includes classroom teachers, bus drivers, specials teachers, custodians, cafeteria staff, social workers, parents, and community members (see p. 38).

"Our students are everyone's responsibility. Each role has value." No one in the school is viewed as a babysitter or an "invisible" cog in the system. Each person is valued and each person is expected to model Be the Solution behavior and messaging for the students.

Recruiting your PE teacher is a great place to start! A 60-second "Be Solution Meditation" written by Awan Blackhawk, the PE teacher, is read to the whole school over the loudspeaker. This is a great opportunity for the teacher to reinforce the Be the Solution behavior that he would like to see in his PE room, such as proper use of equipment or respecting personal space. The principal warmly introduces him, "I am happy to welcome Mr. Blackhawk, our PE teacher, to share his Be the Solution Minute with us this morning." Mr. Blackhawk reads the meditation, and then the principal cues the beginning and ending of activity by announcing, "Your 60 seconds of silence begins/ends now." The principal then thanks "Mr. Blackhawk, for sharing his Be the Solution Minute with Dorothy Adam High School this morning. I agree it is important that we all remember to respect our PE equipment. That equipment was purchased for us all to share and so we must handle it carefully and with respect."

6. Problem: I love using a Call to Action to get students motivated! Can I have a few more examples of **how it can help transitions** when time is tight?

Solution: Room 314 is working in cooperative groups on their poetry posters when the fire alarm goes off. By the time the students return to their classroom, there are only 2 minutes remaining in the period. Mr. Caillou, the teacher, needs the room cleaned up for his next period class.

Mr. Caillou announces, "OK Room 314, it is time to **Be the Solution!**" He moves swiftly to the board and writes the following:

> Be the Solution: Cleaning up after group work
> Time start: 11:04
> Time stop: 11:06

Alternatively, a teacher senses that her classroom is really nervous before a test. She wants them to practice a quick activity to get centered and focused.

> "OK, 6th Period, our class needs to Get **In the Zone** and focus before our exam. Lee Sun Yew, will you select an activity from the POP Chart that will help our class Get In the Zone and focus?" Once the activity has been chosen, the teacher writes the time and activity on the board.

Be In the Zone: Focus for our test

> Activity: Memory Minute
> Time start: 1:02
> Time stop: 1:03

Lee Sun Yew facilitates the activity as the teacher acts as timer.

7. Problem: I need a few more examples of how I can use **both structured and unstructured** movement with my students. Also, I never know what type of music to play for my students. Any ideas?

Solution: Practicing movement prior to group work or a test is a great way to help the class release excess energy that can often make being present and focused challenging for your more frenetic students. For **a structured approach**, lead your students through a sequence of physical movements appropriate for the classroom. You can write a sequence on the board, such as:

10 Jumping Jacks
Tree Pose (5 breaths)
10 Jumping Jacks
Tree Pose (5 breaths)
Seated Arm Stretch (10 breaths)

For **a less structured approach** or when working with a reluctant group, put on music and declare "Hoof It" for the next 90 seconds. Students can move in whatever way they feel comfortable (fast or slow, subtle, or grand), as long as they are respecting their neighbor's personal space and using moves appropriate for school (i.e., no fighting gestures, miming sexual positions, or fake firing of weapons). When you feel the students' energy starting to shift, ask the students slowly find their seats. Once they are seated, close the session with a centering activity like Memory Minute (p. 110).

For music, my Mindful Practices team created a fun Motown playlist to use with student and adult learners. It is upbeat and always a hit!

"I Can't Help Myself" (Four Tops)
"The Way You Do the Things You Do" (The Temptations)
"Superstition" (Stevie Wonder)
"You Can't Hurry Love" (The Supremes)
"Everyday People" (Sly and the Family Stone)
"Please Mr. Postman" (The Marvelettes)
"It's Your Thing" (The Isley Brothers)
"Think" (Aretha Franklin)
"ABC" (The Jackson 5)
"Cool Jerk" (The Capitols)
"Hold On, I'm Coming" (Sam & Dave)
"Knock on Wood" (Eddie Floyd)
"Lovely Day" (Bill Withers)

References and Further Reading

Acedo, C., Opertti, R., Brady, J., and Duncombe, L. (2011). *Interregional and Regional Perspectives on Inclusive Education: Follow-up of the 48th Session of the International Conference on Education*. Paris: United Nations Educational, Scientific and Cultural Organization.

Adams, J. (2017). *The ABC of Mindfulness*. Mindfulnet.org.

Albright, M. I., and Weissberg, R. P. (2010). "School–Family Partnerships to Promote Social and Emotional Learning." In S. L. Christenson and A. L. Reschly (Eds.), *Handbook of School–Family Partnerships*, pp. 246–265. New York: Routledge.

Barrera, Jr., M., Biglan, A., Taylor, T. K., Gunn, B. K., Smolkowski, K., Black, C., Ary, D. V., and Fowler, R. C. (2002). "Early Elementary School Intervention to Reduce Conduct Problems: A Randomized Trial with Hispanic and Non-Hispanic Children." *Prevention Science*, 3(2): 83–94.

Biffle, C. (2013). *Whole Brain Teaching for Challenging Kids (and the Rest of Your Class, Too!)*. Yucaipa, CA: Whole Brain Teaching LLC.

Brown, B. (2010). *The Gifts of Imperfection: Let Go of Who You Think You're Supposed to Be and Embrace Who You Are*. Center City, MI: Hazelden.

Butzer, B., Bury, D., Telles, S., and Khalsa, Sat Bir S. (2016). "Implementing Yoga within the School Curriculum: A Scientific Rationale for Improving Social-Emotional Learning and Positive Student Outcomes." *Journal of Children's Services*, 11(1): 3–24.

Chicago Public Schools (CPS) (2017). *School Quality Rating Policy*. http:// cps.edu/Performance/Pages/PerformancePolicy.aspx.

Collaborative for Academic, Social, and Emotional Learning (CASEL). CASEL.org.

Cook-Cottone, C. P. (2015). *Mindfulness and Yoga for Self-Regulation: A Primer for Mental Health Professionals*. New York: Springer.

Danielson, C., and Chicago Public Schools (CPS) (2011). *CPS Framework for Teaching Companion Guide: Version 1.0*. Chicago: CPS.

Durlak, J. A., Weissberg, R. P., Dymnicki, A. B., Taylor, R. D., and Schellinger, K. B. (2011). "The Impact of Enhancing Students' Social and Emotional Learning: A Meta-Analysis of School-Based Universal Interventions." *Child Development*, 82(1): 405–432.

Farhi, D. (1996). *The Breathing Book: Good Health and Vitality through Essential Breath Work*. New York: Henry Holt.

Farrington, C. A., Roderick, M., Allensworth, E., Nagaoka, J., Keyes, T. S., Johnson, D. W., and Beechum, N. O. (2012). *Teaching Adolescents to Become Learners*, pp. 1–102. Chicago, IL: University of Chicago Consortium on Chicago School Research Literature Review.

Fisher, E. P. (1992). "The Impact of Play on Development: a Meta-Analysis." *Play and Culture*, 5(2): 159–181.

Forbes, H. T. (2013). "Teaching Trauma in the Classroom." *Focus on Adoption*, 21(4): 27.

Friedman, J., and Boumil, M. (1995). *Betrayal of Trust: Sex and Power in Professional Relationships*. Westport, CT: Praeger.

Froh, J., and Bono, G. (2014). *Seven Ways to Foster Gratitude in Kids*. Berkeley, CA: The Greater Good Science Center.

Fullan, M. (2011). *Change Leader: Learning to Do What Matters Most*. San Francisco, CA: Jossey-Bass.

Goleman, D., and Senge, P. (2014). *The Triple Focus: A New Approach to Education*. Florence, MA: More Than Sound.

Greene, R. W. (2014). *Lost at School: Why Our Kids with Behavioral Challenges Are Falling through the Cracks and How We Can Help Them*. New York: Scribner.

Hackney, P. (2002). *Making Connections: Total Body Integration through Bartenieff Fundamentals*. New York: Routledge.

Hargreaves, A., and Fullan, M. (2012). *Professional Capital: Transforming Teaching in Every School*. New York: Teachers College Press.

Harrison, L. J., Manocha, R., and Rubia, K. Sahaja (2004). "Yoga Meditation as a Family Treatment for Children with Attention Deficit–Hyperactivity Disorder." *Clinical Child Psychology and Psychiatry*, 9: 479–497.

Hattie, J. (2009). *Visible Learning: A Synthesis of Over 800 Meta-Analyses Relating to Achievement*. New York: Routledge.

Illinois State Board of Education (ISBE) (n.d.). *Social-Emotional Learning Standards*. ISBE.state.il.us.

Illinois State Board of Education (ISBE) (2006). *Special Education and Support Services: Service Learning Guide*. ISBE.state.il.us.

Illinois State Board of Education (ISBE) (2013). *Illinois Early Learning and Development Standards*. ISBE.state.il.us.

Jennings, P. A., and Greenberg, M. T. (2009). "The Prosocial Classroom: Teacher Social Emotional Competence in Relation to Student and Classroom Outcomes." *Review of Educational Research*, 79(1): 491–525.

Jha, A. P., Krompinger, J., and Baime, M. J. (2007). "Mindfulness Training Modifies Subsystems of Attention." *Journal of Cognitive Affective and Behavioral Neuroscience*, 7: 109–119.

Jones, D. (2007). "Healthy and Smart: Using Wellness to Boost Performance." *Principal Leadership*, 8(4): 32–36.

Jones, S., Bouffard, S., and Weissbourd, R. (2013). "Educators' Social and Emotional Skills Vital to Learning." *Kappan Magazine*, 94(8): 62–65.

Kabat-Zinn, J. (1990). *Full Catastrophe Living: Using the Wisdom of Your Body and Mind to Face Stress, Pain and Illness*. New York: Dell.

Kabat-Zinn, J. (2016). "Awareness Has No Center and No Periphery." *Mindfulness*, 7(5): 1241–1242.

Kripalu Center for Yoga and Health (2015). *Kripalu Yoga in the Schools Curriculum*. Stockbridge, MA: Kripalu.

Lawlor, M. S. (2014). "Mindfulness in Practice: Considerations for Implementation of Mindfulness-Based Programming for Adolescents in School Contexts." *New Directions for Youth Development*, 2014(142): 83–95.

Lemov, D. (2010). *Teach Like a Champion: 49 Techniques That Put Students on the Path to College*. San Francisco, CA: Jossey-Bass.

Linden, W. (1973). "Practicing of Meditation by School Children and Their Levels of Field Dependence-Independence, Test Anxiety and Reading Achievement." *Journal of Consulting and Clinical Psychology*, 41: 139–143.

McKinley, J. (2010). *Raising Black Students' Achievement through Culturally Responsive Teaching*. Alexandria, VA: Association for Supervision and Curriculum Development.

Miller, J. (2015). "The Power of Parenting with Social and Emotional Learning." *Huffington Post*, June 15.

National Child Traumatic Stress Network Schools Committee (2008). *Child Trauma Toolkit for Educators*. Los Angeles, CA, and Durham, NC: National Center for Child Traumatic Stress. www.nctsnet.org/sites/default/files/assets/pdfs/Child_Trauma_Toolkit_Final.pdf.

Nuthall, G. A. (1999). "Learning How to Learn: The Evolution of Students' Minds through the Social Processes and Culture of the Classroom." *International Journal of Educational Research*, 31(3): 141–256.

Patrick, S. D., Tsukayama, E., and Duckworth, A. L. (2014). "A Tripartite Taxonomy of Character." Paper presented at the annual meeting of the American Education Research Association, Philadelphia, PA, April 2014.

Purcell, M., and Murphy, J. (2014). *Mindfulness for Teen Anger*. Oakland, CA: New Harbinger Publications.

Roeser, R. W., and Peck, S. C. (2009). "An Education in Awareness: Self, Motivation, and Self-Regulated Learning in Contemplative Perspective." *Educational Psychologist*, 44(2): 119–136.

Rubin, G. (2011). *The Happiness Project*. New York: HarperCollins.

Senge, P., Cambron-McCabe, N., Lucas, T., Smith, B., Dutton, J., and Kleiner, A. (2012). *Schools that Learn: A Fifth Discipline Fieldbook for Educators, Parents, and Everyone Who Cares About Education*. New York: Crown Business.

Serwacki, M., and Cook-Cottone, C. (2012). "Yoga in the Schools: A Systematic Review of the Literature." *International Journal of Yoga Therapy*, 22(1): 101–110.

Shechtman, N., DeBarger, A., Dornsife, C., Rosier, S., and Yarnall, L. (2013). "Promoting Grit, Tenacity, and Perseverance: Critical Factors for Success in the 21st Century." *U.S. Department of Education Office of Educational Technology*, February 14.

Siegel, R. (2014). *The Science of Mindfulness: A Research-Based Path to Well-Being*. The Great Courses (audio).

Sparrowe, L. (2011). "Transcending Trauma." *Yoga International*, Fall: 48–53 and 89.

Spolin, V. (1986). *Theater Games for the Classroom: A Teacher's Handbook*. Chicago, IL: Northwestern University Press.

Strong, W. B., Malina, R. M., Blimkie, C. J. R., Daniels, S. R., Dushman, R. K., Gutin, B., Hergenroeder, A. C., Must, A., Nixon, P. A., Pivarnik, J. M., Rowland, T., Trost, S., and Trudeau, F. (2005). "Evidence Based Physical Activity for School-Age Youth." *The Journal of Pediatrics*, 146(6): 732–737.

Stueck, M., and Gloeckner, N. (2005). "Yoga for Children in the Mirror of the Science: Working Spectrum and Practice Fields of the Training of Relaxation with Elements of Yoga for Children." *Early Child Development and Care*, 175(4): 371–377.

Tantillo, C., and Crowley, E. (2012). *Cooling Down Your Classroom: Using Yoga, Relaxation and Breathing Strategies to Help Students Learn to Keep Their Cool*. Chicago, IL: Mindful Practices.

Tantillo Philibert, C. (2016). *Everyday SEL in Elementary School*. London: Routledge.

Trauma and Learning Policy Initiative (2013). *Helping Traumatized Children Learn, Volume 2: Creating and Advocating for Trauma-Sensitive Schools*. https://traumasensitiveschools.org/tlpi-publications/download-a-free-copy-of-a-guide-to-creating-trauma-sensitive-schools/.

Van der Kolk, B. (2014). *The Body Keeps the Score*. New York: Penguin Books.

Wessler, S., and Preble, W. (2003). *The Respectful School: How Educators and Students Can Conquer Hate and Harassment*. Alexandria, VA: Association for Supervision and Curriculum Development.

Willard, C. 2014. *Mindfulness for Teen Anxiety*. Oakland, CA: Instant Help Publications.

Wong, H. K. (2009). *Facilitator's Handbook: The Effective Teacher*. Mountain View, CA: Harry K. Wong Publications.

Wong, H. K., and Wong, R. T. (2009). *The First Days of School: How To Be an Effective Teacher*. Mountain View, CA: Harry K. Wong Publications.